soft people

The Art of Dollcrafting

soft people

The Art of Dollcrafting

By

Loretta Pompilio

Drawings Mary A. Scott/Photos Raymond Pompilio

THE CROSSING PRESS / TRUMANSBURG / NEW YORK 14886

Copyright © 1979   Loretta Pompilio

Credits—
Cover: Mary A. Scott, Tom Parker
Book Design: Mary A. Scott
Editorial Assistance: Mary A. Scott, E. Gill, Alice Richardson, J. Lapham
Photo page 21 Ron George

Library of Congress Cataloging in Publication Data

Pompilio, Loretta.
  Soft people.

  I. Dollmaking.   2. Soft toy making.
I. Title.
TTl75.P65   745.59'22   78-10288
ISBN 0-89594-013-2
ISBN 0-89594-0117-5 pbk.

Contents

Introduction

My interest in dolls didn't begin when I was a child. I gave up playing with dolls when I was four years old and, while most of my friends were playing with Ginny dolls which came with lots of clothes in a big plastic box, my best friend and I were playing with sand, creating space cities on Mars.

When I got to high school, there was a clear line drawn between people who took home economics (cooking and sewing) and those who took art classes. I gravitated toward art classes and didn't even take the cover off a sewing machine till I was twenty-one.

Then I began to want to create my own clothes and, though dress patterns were as difficult for me to follow as instructions for putting together a color TV, the desire to make my own clothes won out and I began to use a sewing machine. Later on, I began to embroider the clothes I made, discovering I could create pictures without using a pen or brush. Still later, I realized I could create these pictures more easily by appliqueing swatches of cloth on my clothing. Finally, I learned that a sewing machine could also be used for applique. I went to a course in machine applique and found to my surprise that the teacher was using applique for dollmaking.

From there everything fell into place. I could even make Martians to people the planets of my doll-less childhood.

1

Beginning

Inspiration

I am inspired by anything I see, from a person on the street to a satin dress. You can get inspiration for a doll anywhere. For instance, try to draw one of your friends or family. On the facing page is a drawing I made of my husband and the doll that came from it.

If you feel you can't draw well enough, go to the children's section of the library and look at books with illustrations. You'll be

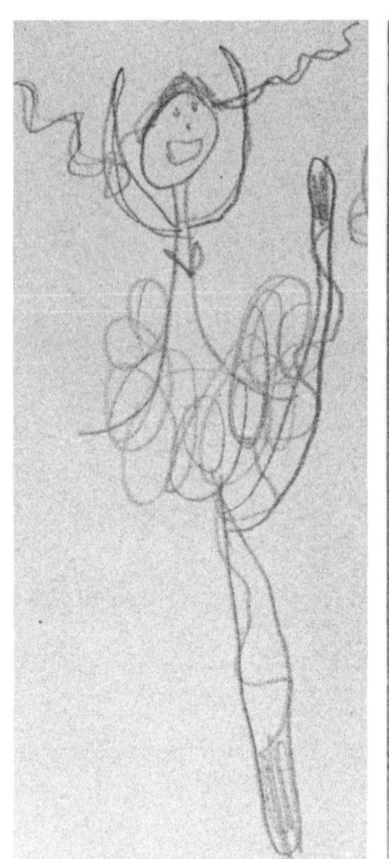

amazed at the fun dolls that are readily available to you. Or ask any child you know to do a drawing of someone for you. Children's drawings are magical. They always see what is really there. To the left are some drawings by young friends of mine and the dolls that resulted.

You also can work from paintings by famous artists, like Renoir or Gauguin. Any of these methods are valid–I didn't always think so until I began to realize that artists always borrow from each other. Feel free to use whatever you find.

Patterns

I give several patterns in this book as well as many techniques. If you feel the need to start with a readymade form, try one or all of these patterns. However, you will notice that, no matter how hard you try, the dolls you make will not look like mine. This is precisely the purpose of this book, to give you a jumping off point. After you make the plunge, I am sure you will realize the many possibilities for original dolls within you. You're welcome to the basic patterns, but please don't be afraid to create your own.

Other Dolls

You can also get inspiration by looking at other dolls. On the following pages is a portfolio of dolls in my collection. I found these dolls at barn sales and craft fairs. A couple were brought to me from foreign countries. All are wonderful, made to be loved and played with. And to make them even more accessible, I've done some very simple, x-ray drawings to indicate how they were put together. I am also enclosing photos of Heidi and Peter, my two earliest dolls, in the hope they may prove useful to you. You're welcome to copy whatever you like.

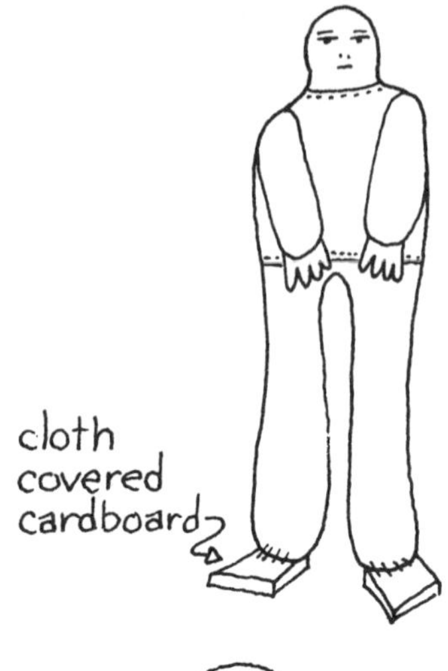

1. An American Indian doll
   - body (head, torso & legs) sewn & stuffed
   - shirt of velvet, sewn to the body
   - arms stuffed & attached to shirt
   - underskirt & overskirt of calico
   - beads handmade by Indians
   - face drawn on peach colored cotton
   - fabric with black & red magic markers
   - hair made of fleece, sewn to head

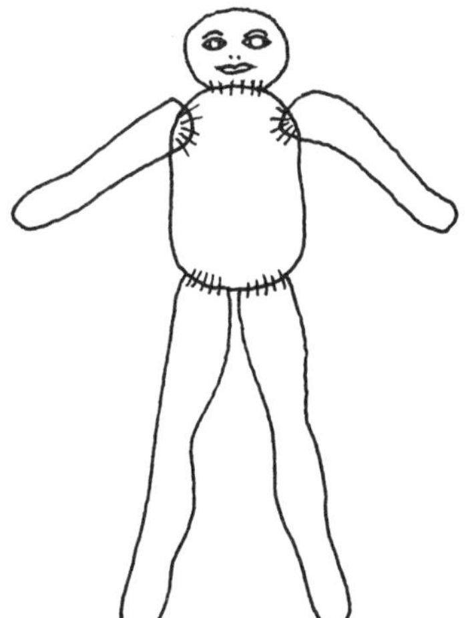

2. Delia, a doll my mother brought me from Ireland
   - body of cotton sateen with limbs sewn on loosely
   - clothing–a green felt skirt sewn to the body & a handknit sweater
   - face, painted & drawn with magic markers
   - hair of yellow wool, stitched to the head
   - not showing, some beautiful lace panties

3. A friend of mine, Dawn Scott, made this doll when she was fourteen years old.
   - body, arms & head in one piece
   - face drawn on peach colored cotton felt with features drawn with black & red magic markers
   - legs made of tubes of herringbone wool with pair of stuffed boots attached
   - hair of homespun wool sewn to head

1
2
3

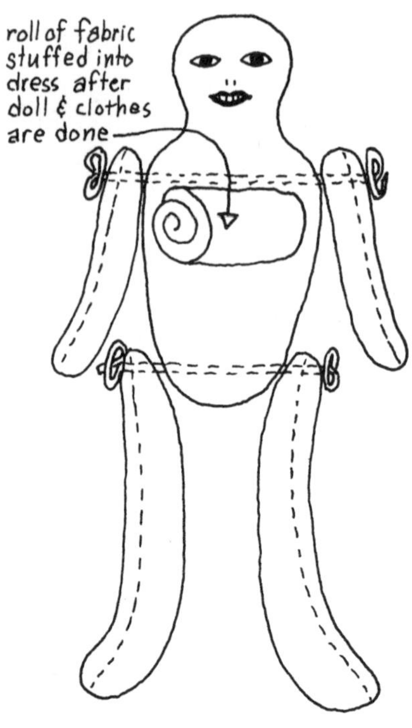

4. This doll is from Nassau
   - body made of black cotton, sewn & stuffed
   - arms & legs, sewn & stuffed, then attached with wire passing through body
   - face black cotton, with features in white & red tempera paint
   - panties & blouse a cotton print, sewn to body
   - skirt made of 2 different printed fabrics pieced together
   - apron of white cotton with waistband serving as skirt band
   - bosom made of stuffing applied over the body & under the blouse
   - hat made of straw with fabric & paper mache fruit

5. The pantaloon doll
   - body has arms & legs attached loosely. They are left unstuffed for half an inch where they are stitched to the body, allowing a lot of movement
   - bosom is padded with stuffing applied over the body & under the blouse
   - dress trimmed with rickrack
   - face painted on with brush
   - hair of yarn, glued on
   - shoes of felt, glued on

4
5
NASSAU

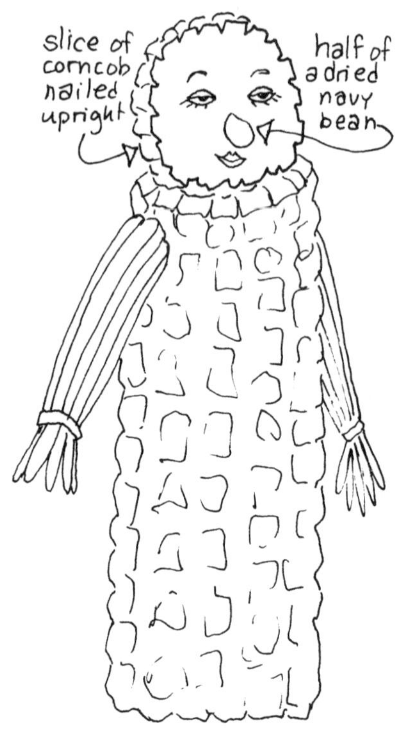

6. A corncob doll
   - body is a corn cob, stripped of corn
   - face sculpted from top of corn cob & painted
   - arms of 5 pipe cleaners put through hole drilled in cob
   - clothing of matching hat & dress.
   - Dress stiff enough so that she can stand by herself

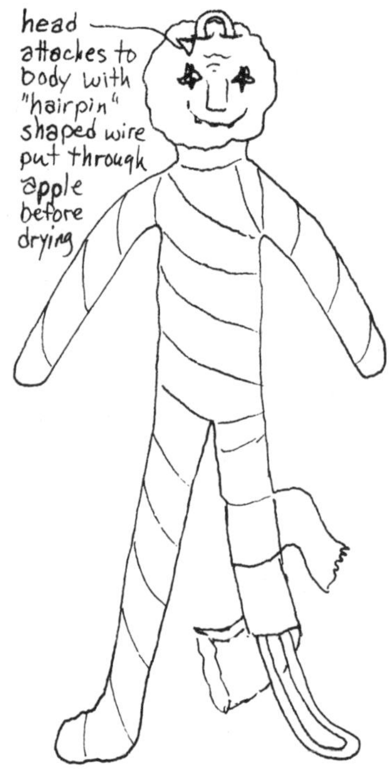

7. Apple head doll
   - head a cooking apple lightly carved & dried; teeth pearl beads & eyes of cloves, all inserted before drying apple
   - body a wire skeleton wrapped with cotton batting & gauze
   - hair homespun yarn glued to apple head
   - underclothes lace trimmed panta-loons & petticoat
   - shoes made of leather, sewn & glued
   - dress made of silk print, sewn on
   - shawl made of lace
   - hat crocheted of white thread

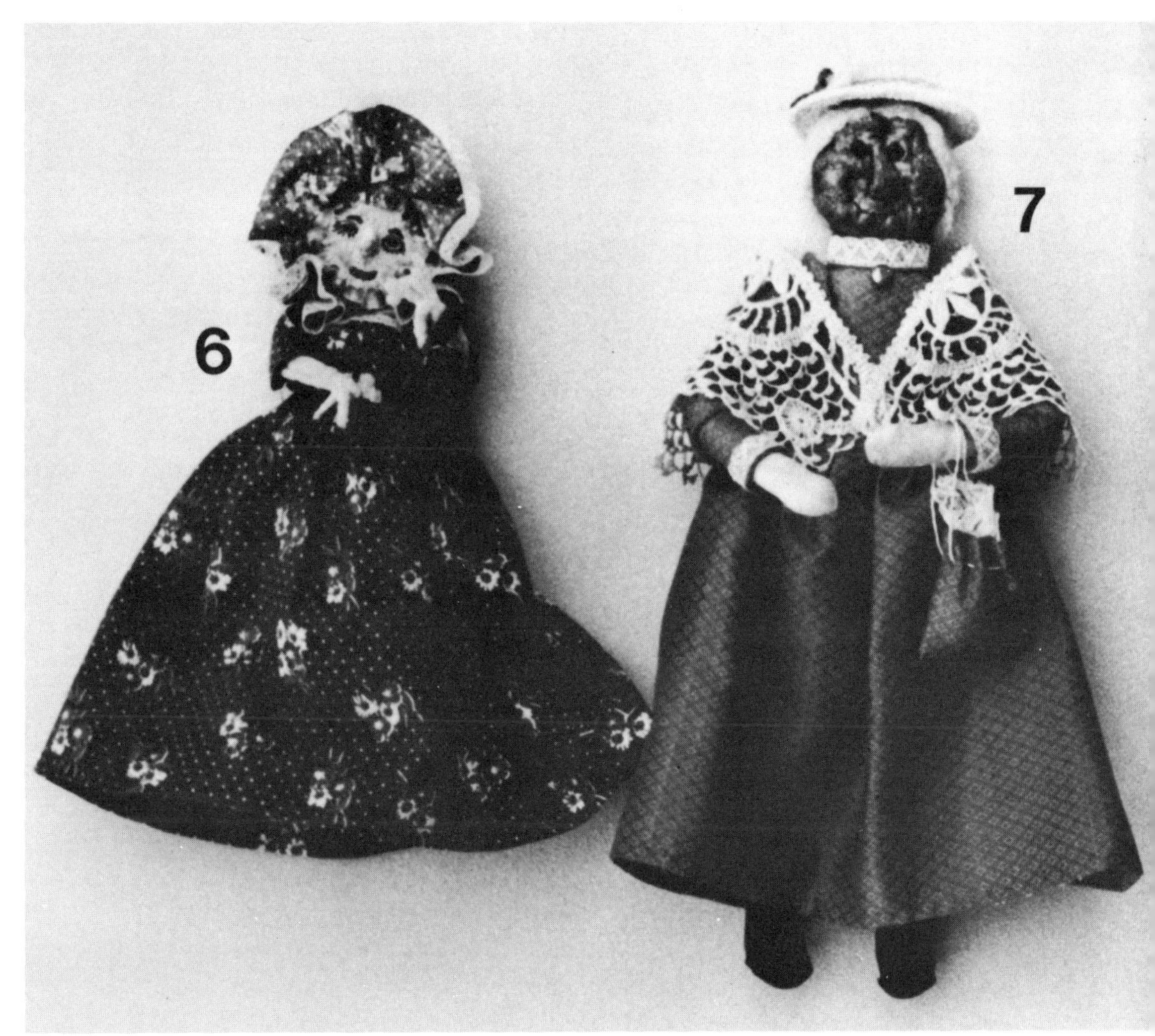

6
7

The following two dolls I found at a barn sale. There is no knowing their ethnic origin. I suspect Eastern Europe but am not sure. The dolls have armatures made of whittled wood with flat disc faces which are covered with fabric and then attached.

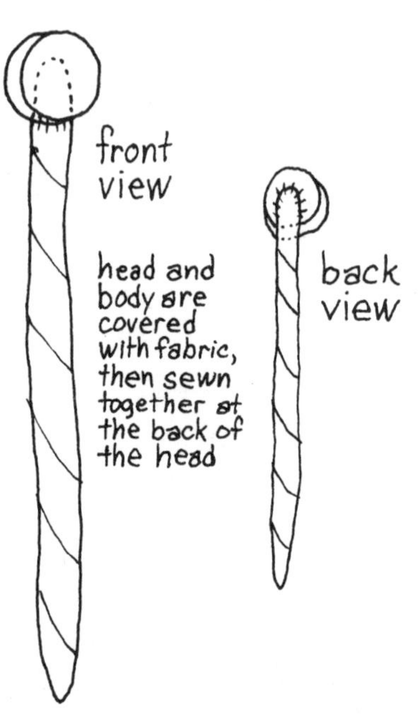

8. The first doll has no arms.
   - face white cloth painted pink with features drawn in soft pencil
   - cap of lace with a net train & gold sequins over forehead & under chin
   - hair brown, of human origin
   - neck wrapped in green cloth with pink neckband
   - skirt of printed cotton with apron of another fabric, tied in back

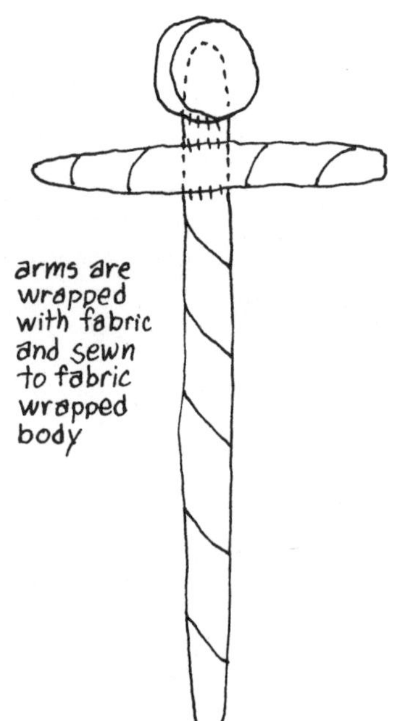

9. The other doll has arms made of a crosspiece of whittled wood much like a popsickle stick.
   - face of coarsely woven white cloth with features drawn in pencil
   - cap of green fabric, edged in gold, with short pink veil
   - small amount of brown human hair
   - neck wrapped in blue & red cloth
   - dress a white & blue kimono with red & blue checked apron

8
9

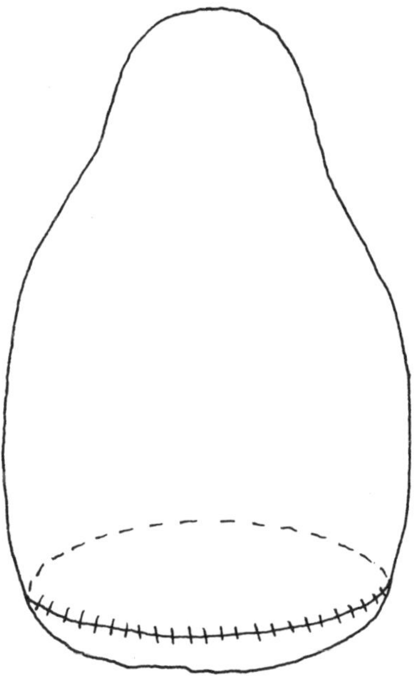

10. Heidi is my very first doll. My children really love her.

- body made of 3 pieces of cloth, the third forming the base, all of pink brushed corduroy
- dress of dark green printed cotton stitched at neck with white lace & bow of yellow cotton rickrack, but not attached at the base
- arms appliqued with pink corduroy
- fingers indicated on arms by 3 embroidered black stitches
- face, embroidery & applique: cheeks of felt, nose embroidered, mouth embroidered felt, eyes appliqued felt, detailed with embroidery
- hair commercially spun black wool sewn in a hoop over top of head

11. Peter is the doll I made in my machine
applique class.
- head & body are constructed of one
  piece of fabric
- face is embroidered
- beard and vest are appliqued
- sleeves and arms are stuffed & sewn on
- boots are also stuffed & sewn on

2

How to Proceed from Drawing to Pattern

You have been inspired to make a doll by a drawing, either one of your own or a child's or an artist's. Whatever the source, you have decided on what your doll will be and you need to transfer the idea to a usable pattern from which the doll can be made.

You will have to take a close look at the drawing and ask yourself several questions. Does the drawing have to be altered to give it a form that can be sewn and stuffed? Is the drawing the same size you want the finished doll to be or does it have to be enlarged or reduced?

Consider how the doll will be displayed. Will it be sitting or standing? Will it be a single shape (standing) or must it sit or bend and therefore have joints?

If the drawing does not have to be altered in any way, if it can be translated to doll form easily, and if it will be a standing form without joints, you can proceed to make your pattern.

A Single Shape Pattern

Lay the drawing flat, face up. Place a piece
of tracing paper over the top. With a heavy
pencil or felt tipped pen, trace the outline
of the drawing onto the tracing paper.

> **Note**: If the original drawing is already
> on heavy paper and there is no need to
> keep it intact, you may use it for your
> pattern, thus eliminating the need to
> transfer it.

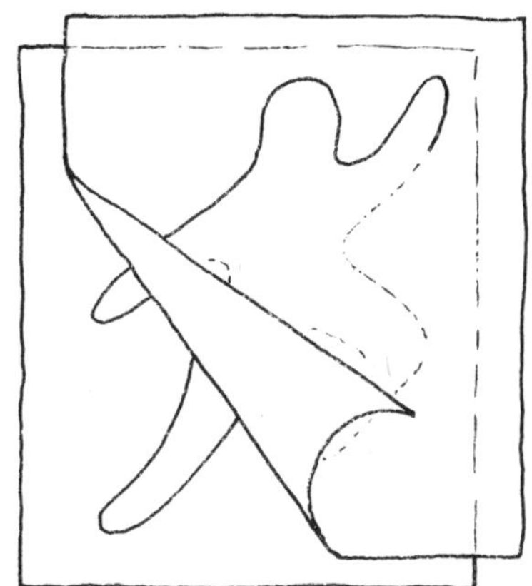

Then transfer the outline from the tracing
paper to heavy paper by inserting a piece
of carbon paper face down between the
two. Using a pencil or ball point pen, repeat the drawing.

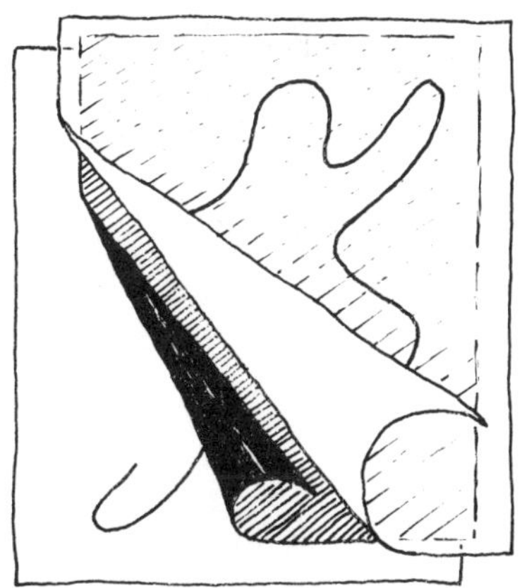

Draw a second line ½" outside the outline.
> **Important**: The actual stitching line is
> ¼" in from this second line. The other
> ¼" is to allow for fabric taken up
> when stuffing. If you do not allow
> extra fabric for stuffing, your finished
> doll will be smaller than you had
> intended.

Your single shape pattern is now complete
and you may proceed by following the
general instructions in the next chapter.

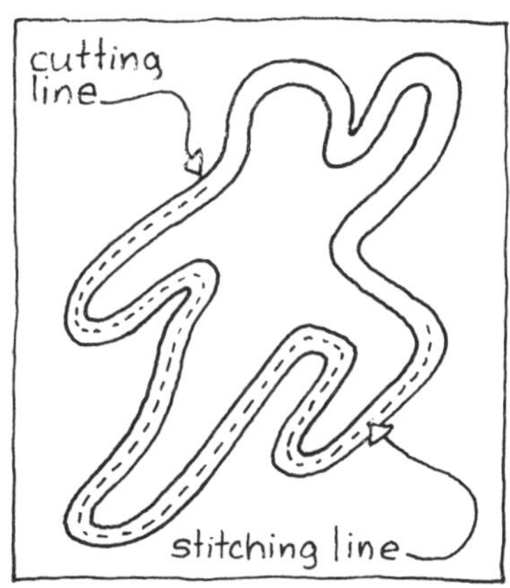

If, on the other hand, the drawing must be altered, read on.

To Alter a Drawing

Various parts of the drawing may need to be simplified or altered so that it can be sewn and stuffed. Place tracing paper over the drawing. Using a dark pencil or felt tipped pen, rework the areas that need to be changed. In this child's drawing, the neck and arms were indicated by a single stroke. When the pattern for the doll was made, these areas were thickened. In addition, the neck and head were simplified to allow greater ease in sewing and to give more strength at the neck. If the outline for the neck had been left slender, the head would have been floppy. Notice, though, that when the neck was drawn on the doll with a pen, the original thinness was retained.

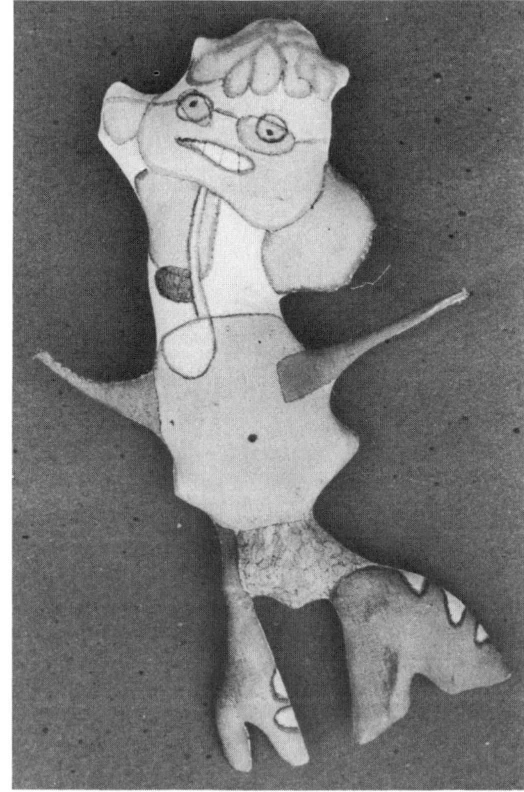

To Enlarge or Reduce a Drawing

First determine how big a doll you want. Is it smaller or larger than the drawing? The quickest way to enlarge or reduce a drawing is to let a machine do it for you. Many xeroxing stores have machines that can alter the size of an image for about a dime apiece.

Another method you can use at home is to use corresponding grids. You draw a series of lines across the drawing, from side to side and from top to bottom, making equal sided squares all over the drawing. If the drawing is expendable, make the grid right on it. If it is something you want to keep, trace it and make the grid on the tracing paper. Then on another sheet of paper you make a similar grid of a proportionally larger size, or use graph paper with appropriately sized squares. If, for example, you want the doll twice as high and twice as wide as the drawing, make the squares twice as large.

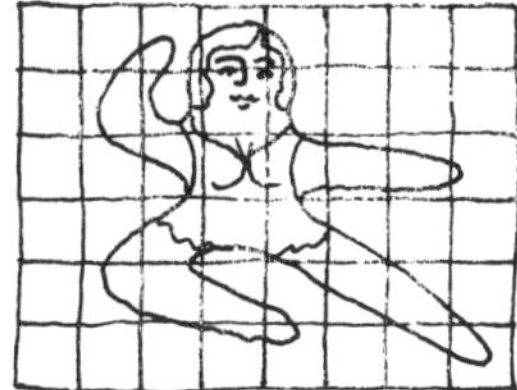 

To transfer the design, carefully copy the drawing from the original grid square by square.

Reverse the process to make the pattern smaller. Instead of larger squares, make smaller squares on a corresponding grid, in proportion to the amount of reduction wanted. Then copy from the original grid, square by square.

Appendages

(Requiring Joints)

Appendages are legs, boots, arms or wings which must be cut, sewn and stuffed separately and added to the trunk later. Please refer to the directions for a single shape pattern above for the general procedure in making a pattern piece.

Place tracing paper over drawing. Trace off the outline of the main body. Then trace off the outline of the appendage. Keep in mind that if you have a right arm or leg and a left arm or leg which are the same shape, only one pattern piece needs to be made. But if they differ, for instance if the right leg is straight whereas the left leg bends, a separate pattern piece will have to be made for each leg.

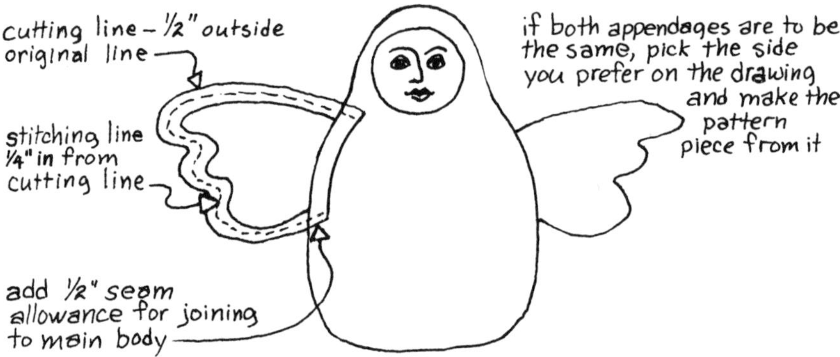

Transfer outline(s) to heavy paper by using carbon paper.

To Add Applique Details

You should decide how you want to apply details. Will facial features and clothing be drawn and painted directly on the body? Or will you "dress" the doll by applying different fabrics to the body? Perhaps the main body fabric will serve as the clothing and it will be necessary to attach separate pieces of fabric that will serve as face and hands. Do you want the doll to be holding anything?

It is not necessary to have patterns for every item that is to be applied over the main trunk. Size and shape can be determined while you are in the process of making the doll. However, if the item has a definite shape or, if you feel more comfortable using a pattern as a guide, make a separate pattern piece.

Place tracing paper over drawing and trace off outline of main body. Transfer to heavy paper using carbon paper. Then trace off the outline of the item to be appliqued and transfer to heavy paper. Add ¼" all around. This will be turned under when the piece is being pinned and stitched to the body. Add ½" where the piece will be sewn in with the main body seam.

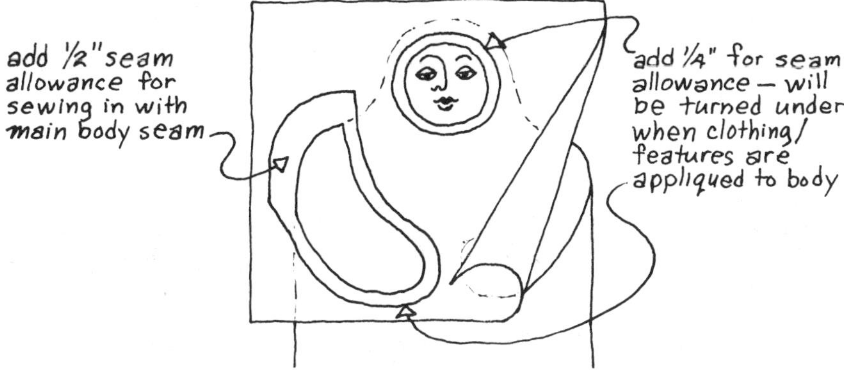

To Make a Pattern Symmetric

If the shape of right and left sides are the same, after your pattern has been completed on heavy paper, fold pattern in half. Pick the side you prefer and cut through both thicknesses of paper, following the outer line of the preferred side. Unfold and you have your pattern.

3

How to Proceed from Pattern to Doll

You have your pattern, either derived from this book or a drawing. You should then select your fabric(s). If the doll is to have features and clothing painted on, I use unbleached muslin for two reasons: it is flesh colored and it is easy to work with. However, you may want to use sheeting or peach or sand colored cloth.

If the doll is to have clothing appliqued or any assortment of different colored appendages, I search my box of scrap fabric and lay out an assortment of fabrics on the pattern to see if they coordinate or clash in an interesting way. Any kind of cloth is useful: velvets, brocades, calicos, denims. For trims, use lace, ribbon, rickrack, buttons, beads, feathers, jewels. Please keep in mind that if the doll is intended for a child, detachable items such as buttons or beads should not be used.

Here are general instructions for a simple two piece doll. For more complex details, see Chapter 4.

To Use Patterns in this Book

Several patterns in this book are actual size. To remove them without cutting the pages, place a sheet of tracing paper over the pattern and with a dark pencil or felt tip pen, copy the outline of the pattern to tracing paper. To transfer the pattern from tracing paper to heavy paper, insert a piece of carbon paper face down between tracing paper and heavy paper. Use a pencil or ball point pen to get a sharp image on the heavy paper. If you do not have carbon paper, use a soft lead pencil and rub a layer of graphite on the reverse side of the tracing paper. Place over heavy paper and trace outline.

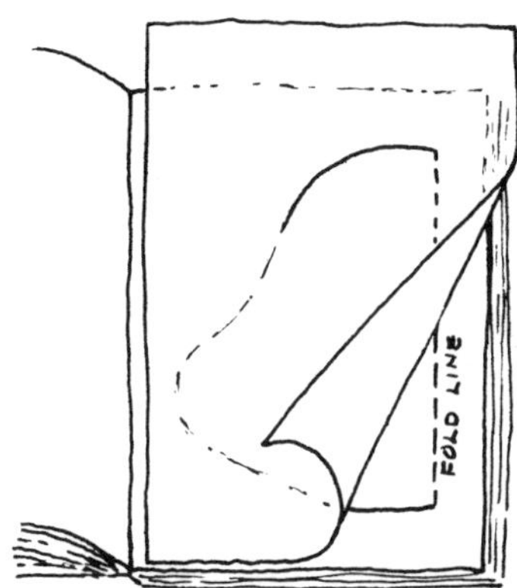

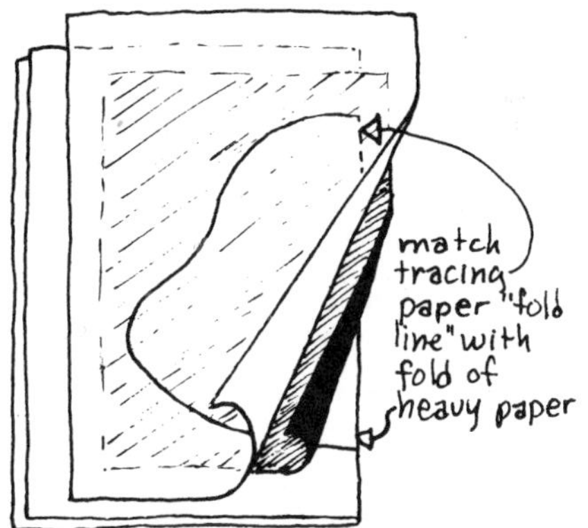

If one side of the pattern in the book states "Place on fold," before transferring the outline to heavy paper, fold the paper in half. Place the tracing paper on the heavy paper, matching the fold line of tracing paper with the fold of the heavy paper. Put carbon paper face down between the two. Trace the outline. With the heavy paper still folded, cut around outline. Open the paper. Pattern is now complete.

To Enlarge or Reduce a Pattern

The easiest method is to use corresponding grids. A complete discussion of them can be found on page 25. The patterns in this book that need to be enlarged are already marked off in small squares. The measurement needed for enlargement is given. If the pattern states, "Each square equals one inch," each square on the larger grid should measure one inch. Unless you have graph paper marked with the grid needed for enlarging the original pattern, you will need to draw your own. Working from left to right, mark off as many large squares as are on the small grid. Repeat down the side. Draw horizontal and vertical lines to complete the grid.

To transfer the enlarged design, carefully copy the outline from the original grid, square by square.

Reverse the process to make the pattern smaller. Instead of larger squares, make smaller squares on a corresponding grid, in proportion to the amount of reduction wanted. Then copy from the original grid, square by square.

A Simple Two Piece Doll

Note: All embroidery, applique and quilting are done while the doll is still flat before front and back are sewn together. Appendages (arms, legs, wings) are added before sewing back and front together. If you are going to have a crease joint, its location must be determined before you sew back and front together. The location of the opening left for stuffing is decided by the crease joint.

Pin pattern to fabric. When back and front are the same fabric, fold fabric in half with right sides together and pin pattern to fabric. If front and back are different fabrics, take two pieces, place right sides together and pin pattern to fabric.

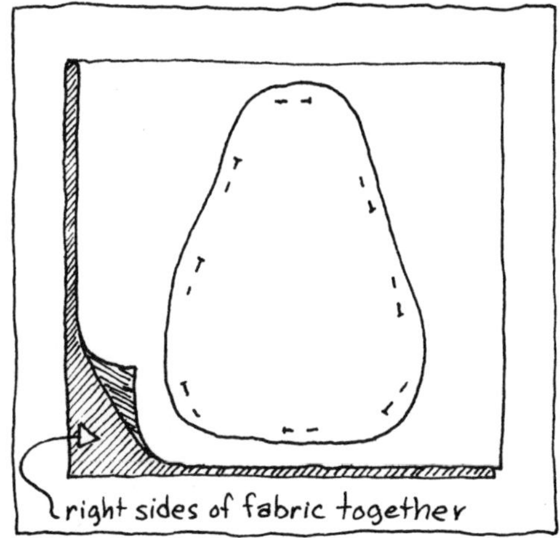

Cut fabric. Use sharp scissors. Cut through fabric along cutting line of pattern.

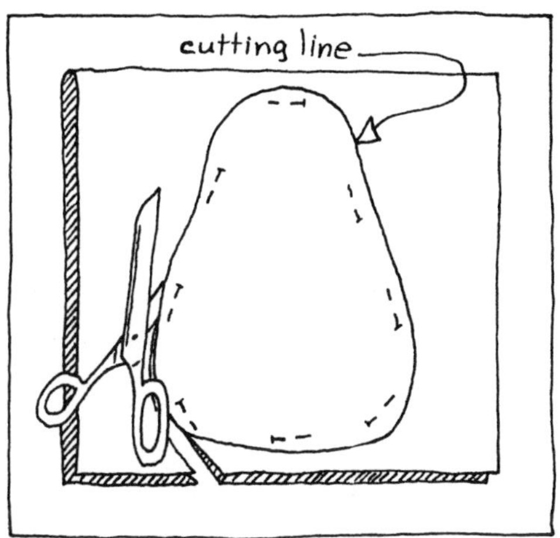

Pin fabric with right sides together. Insert pins at right angles to raw edges.

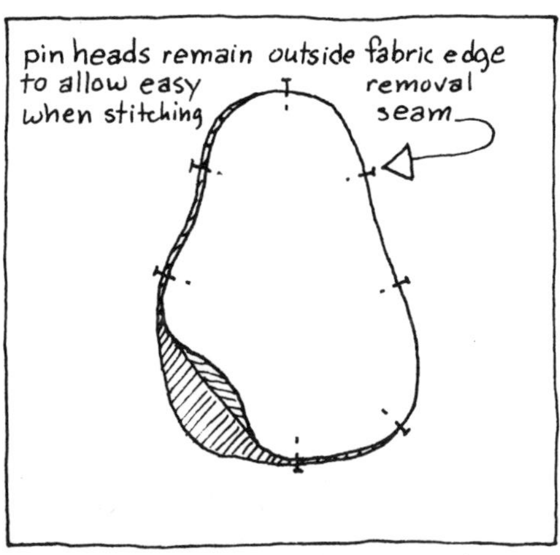

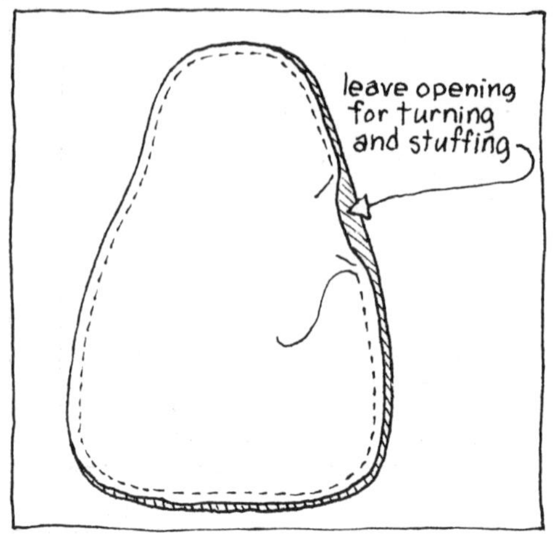

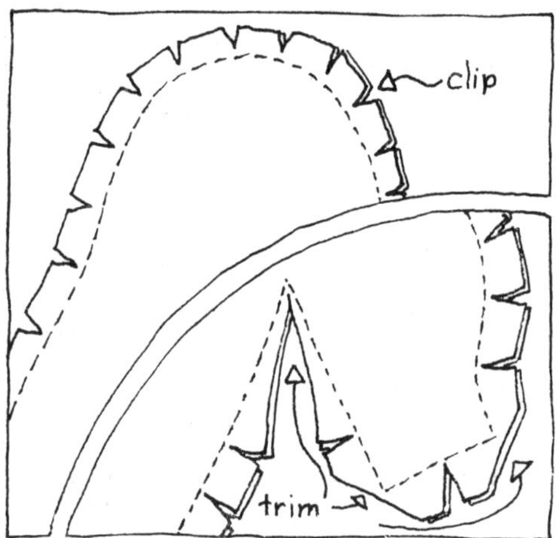

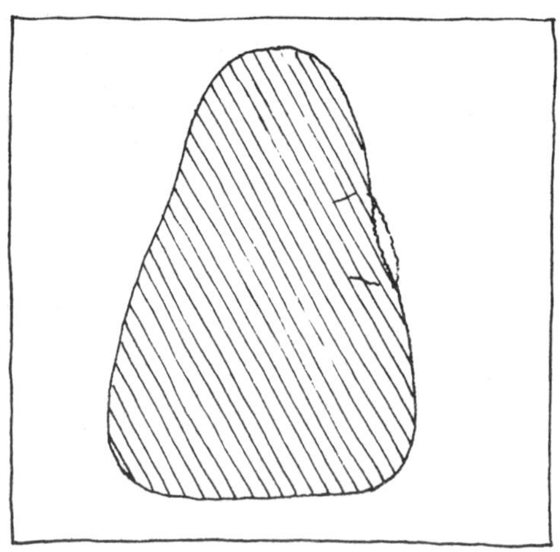

Sew with a machine along seam line (¼" in from raw edge). Be sure to secure stitches at beginning and end by reverse sewing for several stitches. To hand sew, use back-stitch (page 37). Leave a 1" to 2" opening for turning and stuffing. When stitching around curves, go very slowly so that you get an even curve. Sometimes I sew only one stitch at a time, releasing the press-er foot and turning the fabric by hand. When you release the presser foot, be sure the needle remains in the fabric so that you keep an even stitching line.

Clip seams. With a pair of sharp scissors clip almost to the seam every ½". This is especially impor-tant around curves as it allows for the curve to bend, thus giving shape and smoothness when the form is turned. On corners and sharp angles, it is necessary to trim seams.

Turn to reverse fabric and pull through opening.

> **Note:** If you are going to have a crease joint, please see sec-tion on crease joints on page 41,42 before you start stuffing.

Stuff small amounts of fiberfill through opening. Use an eraser end of a pencil or a crochet hook to get into tight areas. Anything smaller may pierce the fabric. Keep in mind the final shape you want in the doll: how the knees should turn, so on. Be careful to stuff with the right quantity of fiberfill--too much fill and the stuffing will migrate through the seams and cause the doll to be hard or stiff. Too little will give the flesh no tone and cause the doll to be floppy.

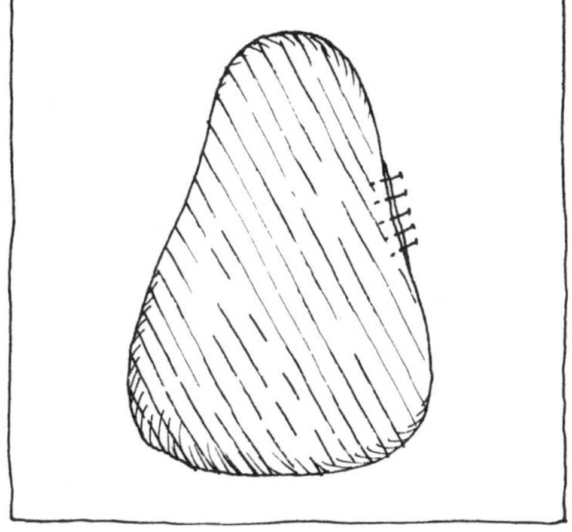

Close opening. Turn raw edges of opening inside along ¼" seam line. Pin closed. Sew the opening closed, using very small stitches. Either of these two stitches are fine:

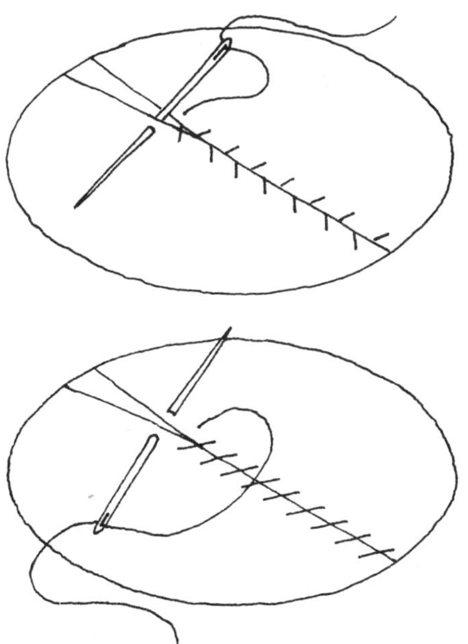

4

Various Techniques Used in Dollmaking

Drawing Features and Clothing

Use a technical fountain pen and black India ink (Mars is fine). If you aren't sure of your skill in drawing, take a scrap of muslin and practice.

With a pen you can also indicate the pattern of the cloth, checks, hearts, polka dots, anything. You can also put on gloves, or shoes, or jewelry.

Painting a Face

You can paint a doll at the beginning when the pieces are flat or you can wait until the very last minute. I prefer waiting until the last moment. There are two methods you can use.

1. Make a transparent wash (ink + water) with russet colored Higgins India ink. Dilute the ink a bit at a time, so that you can

control the intensity of the color. Keep testing the wash by brushing a bit of it on a scrap of muslin. When you have achieved what you want, color cheeks, lips and eyebrows. You may want to add more color to cheeks. I sometimes color the eyes with straight (undiluted) ink.

2. Or you can buy textile paints instead of India ink. Versitex is a good brand, obtainable at an artists' supply store. With textile paints you will have to mix colors to get a flesh tone. Unless you keep exact records, there will be variation in skin color from one doll to the next. But that's okay--you will notice that people come in different colors too!

After you've mixed the paints and obtained a flesh tone you like, add lots of water to it and test with a scrap of the same material you will be using for the face. With a clear brush, wet the parts of the face you will be painting. Put a small amount of paint on a dry brush and apply to face. Start with lips as a test area and then add more or less paint for the cheeks, eyes, so on. You have to iron Versitex to set it. The Versitex package should give you precise directions as to setting of your iron. You can iron the doll after it is stuffed.

Please be as relaxed as possible when you are painting a doll's face. Remember it's all play. If you aren't ready to paint the face, just fool around with pieces of scrap muslin. If you come up with a good face on a piece of scrap, you have the beginning of another doll. You just can't lose.

Painting a Body

Use the paints or inks indicated above, mixed and diluted as you please.

To paint designs on the body, make the designs and the background different colors, or paint the background and leave the design muslin colored, or paint the design and leave the background unpainted. The designs, of course, can be anything: polka dots, hearts, flowers, etc.

You can fill in the outline you have made for shoes or gloves. Remember, after you have applied the paint to your satisfaction, it must be set with an iron.

Embroidery

With embroidery you can do a lot. You can indicate jewelry or clothing, facial features or large areas of color. You can also fasten down fabric with embroidery stitches. Since embroidery is done with the fabric held taut with an embroidery hoop or on a sewing machine, you must embroider while the pieces of your doll are still flat.

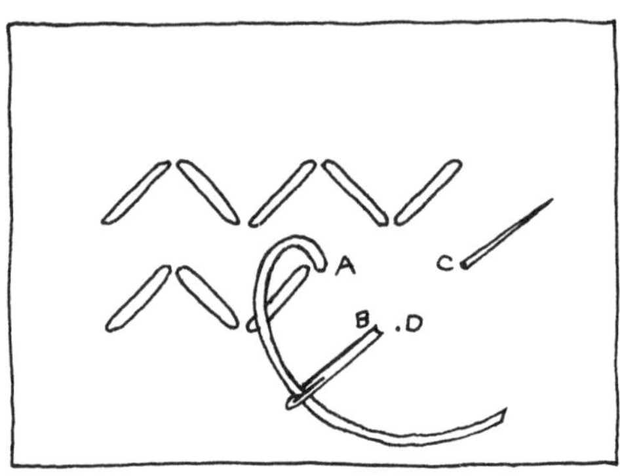

ARROW HEAD STITCH: Use for medium lines and lightly filled areas. Work from left to right. Bring thread up at A. Insert needle at B and bring back up at C. Then insert needle next to B at D.

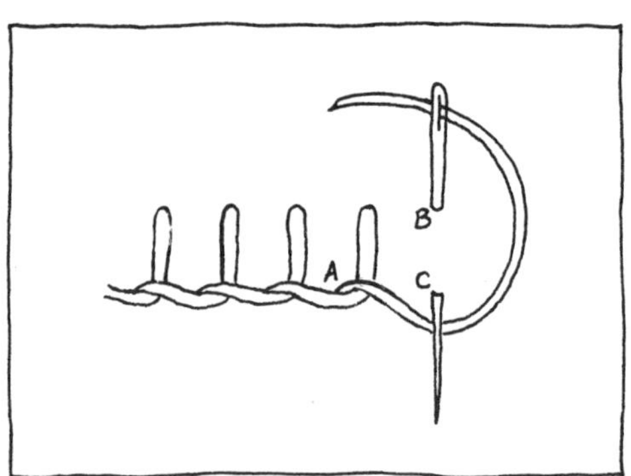

BLANKET STITCH: Use on a raw or a turned edge. Work from left to right. Bring thread up at point A. Hold thread with your thumb, insert needle at B, bring up at C. Needle should go *over* thread under thumb. Repeat. End off securely.

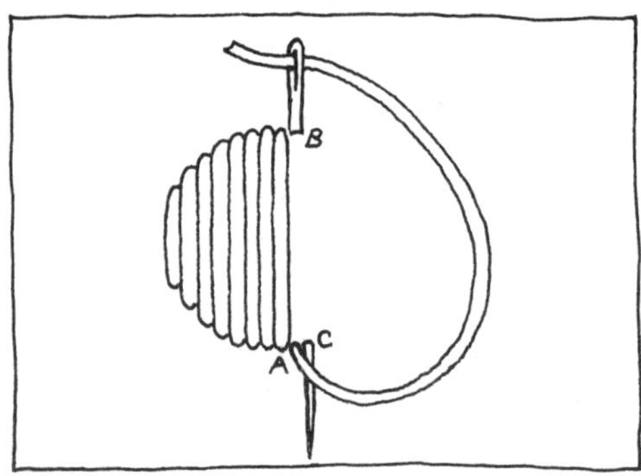

SATIN STITCH: Used to cover a solid area. Bring thread up at A on edge of area to be covered. Insert needle at B on opposite edge and bring up at C, directly next to A. Repeat. Make sure stitches lie side by side, close together.

BACKSTITCH: This is what a sewing machine does. In embroidery it is used for outlining. Stitches are evenly spaced, worked from right to left. Knot your thread and bring it through from back to front (A) so that knot will be on back side where it won't show. Insert needle at point B and bring up at C, left of A. Insert needle at A and bring up at D. Repeat. Be sure to keep the stitches the same length. End off securely by taking three small stitches in the same place.

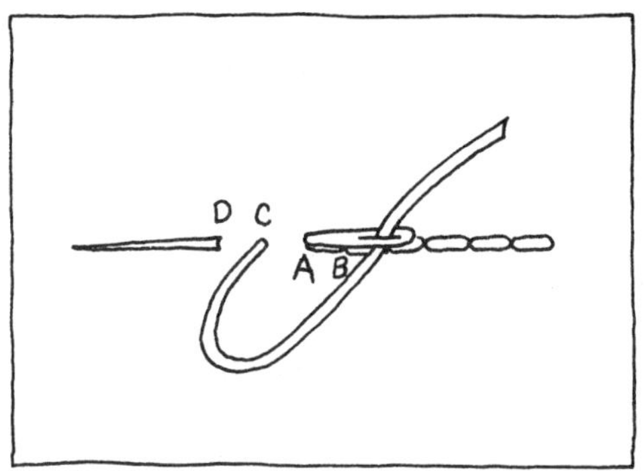

Applique

This is the technique of sewing a piece of fabric on to a contrasting background. I use this method to dress my dolls. You can make the joining of one piece of fabric to another obvious and decorative with embroidery stitches or you can make it unobtrusive with the use of a sewing machine. I myself use a sewing machine. The process: I choose a variety of fabrics that I think will go with a doll's personality and then lay them out on the pattern before I cut them to make sure they coordinate or clash in an interesting way. Then I cut them according to my pattern. I always attach these pieces while the doll is flat. Besides using this process for clothing, I use it for arms or hands on a simple shaped doll. Applique can also be lightly stuffed with fiberfill to give a three dimensional look. (see trapunto)

LACE AS APPLIQUE

Most lace, commercial or handmade, has a motif in flowers, leaves or a geometric pattern. These motifs can be cut out and used as spot appliques on your dolls. If you are using handmade lace, be sure to secure edges where your lace could unravel as cutting usually severs the threads which hold the lace together. It is very difficult for me to cut handmade lace. So much time and often love is put into creating it, I prefer to use it whole whenever possible.

Quilting

This is a method of attaching and holding in place a layer of filling between two layers of fabric. This raises the fabric, giving it shape and dimension. I use it on dolls' faces and hands.

QUILTING A FACE

Measure the diameter of the doll where the face will be. Add ¼" for hemming and cut a circle of unbleached muslin. Draw or embroider the facial features on the muslin circle. You can paint it now or wait until it is sewn on the doll. If you are feeling uncertain about your drawing capabilities, practice on the muslin before cutting. When you have a face that satisfies you, cut your circle out.

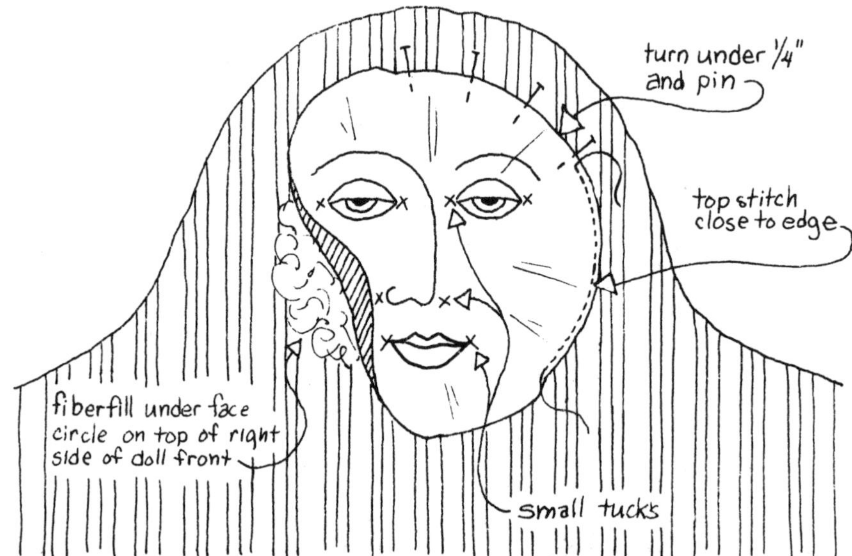

Take a small wad of fiberfill and pin it to the underside of the muslin, pins on top side. Pin circle of muslin and fiberfill to the doll. Is it positioned correctly? Turn raw edges of circle under ¼" and pin. Stitch to doll by hand or machine as close to the edge as possible. If you are using your machine, sew very slowly so you can control the turning. Remove pins as you go.

To add dimensions to the face, take small tucks (stitches) at the corners of the eyes, nose and mouth. **Note**: Tucks of this sort can be used elsewhere on the body or clothing to give a 3 dimensional look.

QUILTING HANDS

I like the hands on my dolls to be holding something and have great fun deciding what the item will be. Some hold flowers, kittens, vegetables, gloves--all kinds of things. The more preposterous the item, the more delighted I am. Consider the effect of a lady dressed in velvet eating a fudge sundae! The hands of my dolls are always small in proportion to the rest.

If the doll has appliqued sleeves, keep in mind that the hands must appear to be coming out of the sleeves. For a doll with both hands together, made in one piece, measure between the ends of the sleeves to determine the size of the piece you need. For a doll with two separate hands, measure the width of the opening of each sleeve and cut a piece for each hand.

Next draw the hands and item to be held on muslin. Practice if you need to until you are satisfied. Take a second piece of muslin. Place behind first piece and sandwich two layers of quilt batting between them. To quilt the hands, use the outline of the hands and the item held for a guide in stitching through the layers of muslin and

batting. Then sew a seam around entire piece and trim next to the seam. Place the hands on the body. If your doll has sleeves, place the hands over the sleeves. Is the positioning believable? Move the piece around a bit until you find the correct placement. Then pin the hands in place and sew to doll, stitching as close to the edge as possible. To complete the hands, add a ruffle of lace where the wrists come from the sleeves. This helps unite the arm and hand.

Trapunto

(Italian Quilting)

If the raised area is higher than in ordinary quilting, it is called Italian quilting or trapunto. See Chapter 10 for examples of trapunto. In order to make these high relief designs, outline the shape you want raised with a running stitch or back stitch and fill it with fiberfill from the back. If the area you are working on is small, you may need a slender stick or crochet hook to push the fiberfill in.

The following directions are for sleeves or arms, but the method would be the same for other items.

SLEEVES/ARMS

For the sleeves, I usually use a piece of contrasting fabric. If the body is solid colored, I use a print or vice versa. If you are not using a pattern, determine the size by measuring the body from shoulder to wrist. Add about an inch to the length and ½" to the width for turning under and for the shoulder seam. With right sides of fabric together, cut two rectangles. Round off the wrist ends and position on body front. Be sure the sleeves' fabric extends at least ½" beyond

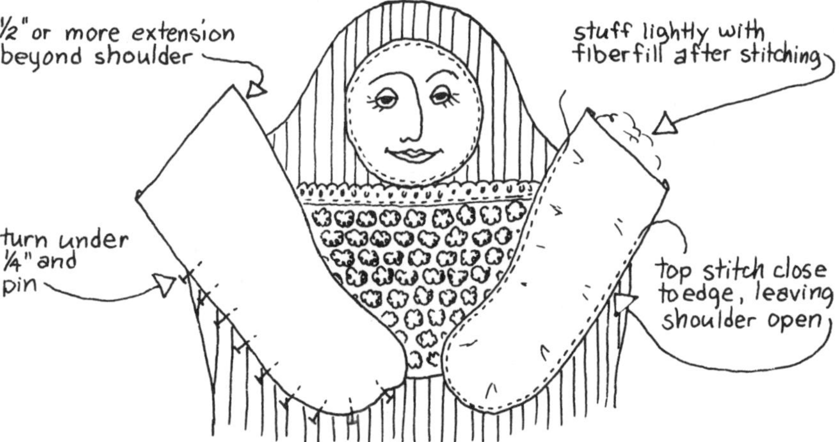

shoulder. Turn raw edges under ¼" and pin around sleeve, leaving shoulder open for stuffing. Sew. After all other work that needs to be done while doll is still flat is completed, lightly stuff sleeves with fiberfill. Appendages, if any, can be added at this time and the back and front sewn together.

Attaching Appendages

(Boots, Wings, Arms and Legs)

An appendage is a part of the doll that is sewn separately and then attached to doll body when the front and back of the body are sewn together. It is made almost in the same manner that a simple two-piece doll is made. Please refer to these basic instructions on page 30.

Fold fabric with right sides together and cut two pair. When sewing fabric together, the opening you leave for stuffing is the same edge you will use to attach appendage to body. Clip seams, trimming where necessary. Turn inside out and stuff, leaving ¾" at top for attaching. After all applique, etc., on front of body is complete, you

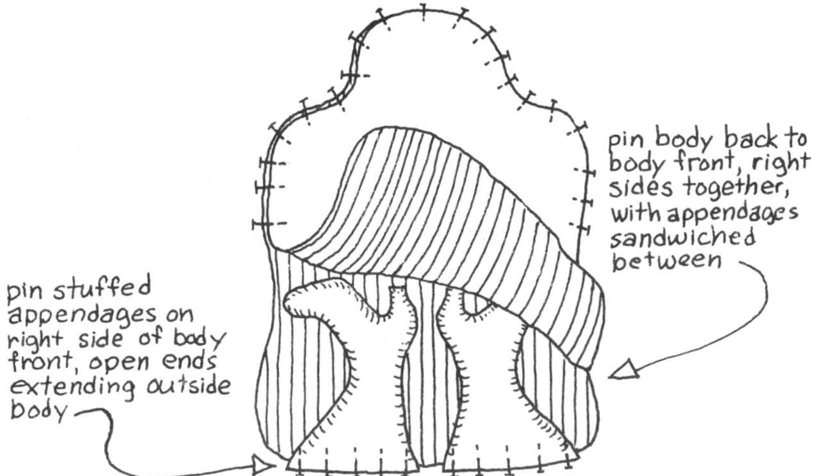

are ready to attach appendages. Lay the body front flat, face up. Place appendages on body. The raw open ends will extend beyond the body on the outside. When they are in position, pin them to the body. Next pin the body back to the body front. Appendages should be sandwiched between the back and the front. Now you are ready to sew the body together.

Crease Joints

There are two types of joints that I use on my dolls. The first is made when an appendage is attached to the body, thus allowing that appendage to move or bend. The second is a crease joint. A crease

joint is made by sewing a seam through both the back and front pieces.
It can be used to make a lap, which allows a doll to sit. In an arm, it
can let an elbow bend and in a leg it can make a knee or foot bend.
In the body, the location must be determined before the front and
back are sewn together as it decides the general location of the opening you leave for stuffing. The actual crease seam is sewn in while you
are stuffing. The procedure is as follows: the location of the crease
joint has been decided. You are ready to stuff. From bottom up, stuff
with fiberfill to the crease line. Then with thread that matches the
fabric, sew the crease seam through both back and front, creating a
joint. Then finish stuffing and close opening.

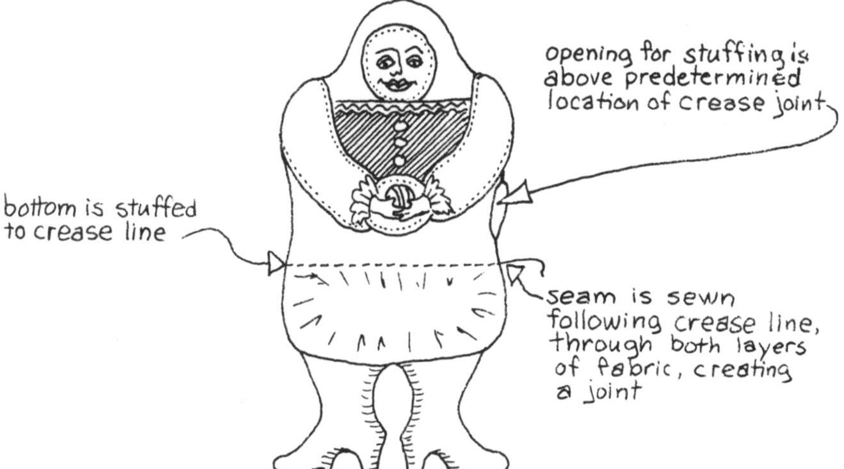

Note: Further development for these techniques may be found in
the instructions for specific dolls.

Hair

Hair-dos are really important to a doll's personality. Think of
the people you know and how different their faces look with any
change of hair style. So play around with different materials, styles
and colors.

FLEECE
(Unspun Wool)

One good hair material is fleece. When using fleece, you will
find there are many different types. One way to categorize fleece is
by the crimp. Crimp is the amount of wave each strand has. I mainly

use Corriedale which has an even crimp. This gives a doll's hair a tufted, wispy look when used in small amounts. Larger amounts give a circus clown effect.

Lincoln is another type of fleece I like for hair. It has a much looser, almost curly crimp and a longer strand. This is very nice on larger dolls as it produces long curly locks.

A third fleece is Romney. The strands are long and somewhat straight, which also produces a nice effect.

I buy any dark fleece I can find regardless of the type and use it either dyed or undyed. A dark black fleece is usually a mixture of black, grey and white wool; when a fleece is dyed, some wonderfully subtle, earthy colors are obtained.

YARN AND OTHER FIBERS

In addition to fleece, there is a variety of yarn and fibers that can be used for hair. You may prefer to purchase yours from local discount stores or supermarkets, or you may wish to use something more exotic (and usually much more expensive) such as mohair, which is very soft and fluffy. You could also try baling twine, jute, kite string, sisal, used rope—even steel wool if the doll is a showpiece rather than a play toy. Consider too cotton balls, fiberfill stuffing, fake and real fur, and torn or shredded fabric. Wrinkled fabric, crochet and knitted pieces can also be tacked down on the doll's head to make interesting hair-dos. These suggestions are only a few of the endless possibilities.

Dying Fleece

I buy white fleece by the piece and then dye it to get exactly the color I want. I either dye a bit of fleece in a small pot, enough for the hair of one or two dolls, or do a large quantity and keep it in stock so that I always have a selection on hand.

Caution: Dyes are poisonous–they can be absorbed either through the lungs or skin. Therefore, be *extremely* careful. Don't breathe over the pot. Stand a respectful distance away and use a wooden stick for stirring. Work outdoors if you can, over a camp stove. If you must work indoors, use a stove which has a hood with a vent leading outside. Wear rubber or surgical gloves. Surgical gloves are better--they give you more freedom of action.

WHAT POT AND UTENSIL TO USE

Pick a pot that is expendable. Enamel and stainless steel are best, although the stainless is more expensive. Cast iron is also suitable, but it "saddens" or dulls the color. Never use aluminum as it combines chemically with the dyes to produce unpredictable colors. It is probably best to go out and buy a cheap enamel pot and earmark it for this purpose only.

Important: Never cook in a pot that has been used for dying.

For small quantities, a pint or quart size pot is fine. For large quantities, use a big soup pot or canning pot.

For utensils, stainless steel and wood are best but stainless implements are expensive. It is probably best to buy cheap, long-handled wooden spoons or get a clean stick from the yard. Never use these utensils for any other purpose except dying.

SMALL QUANTITY DYING

When you are dying fleece in small quantities, it's best to use the dye as it comes from the box, rather than mix colors. Pick the color you want for the hair and proceed as follows:

Put the dye in the water in the proportions indicated on the box. Stir and bring the temperature to lukewarm. Put a small piece of

fleece into the dye bath, but be careful the water isn't too hot. Fleece
can go into shock and felt if it is placed in very hot water. Felting is
what happens when you wash a wool sweater in very hot water; the
fibers shrink and mat together in a tight, thick rug. Of course, if you
want the doll's hair felted as a special effect, that's fine. Just be careful to get the look you want.

After a few minutes, check the color of the fleece. Is it intense
enough? If not, raise the temperature gradually until you get exactly
the color you want. Take the fleece out of the dye bath, rinse it first
with warm water and then with cooler water until the water is clear.
Always make temperature changes very gradually to avoid shock. Dry
the fleece on a piece of newspaper or outside in the sun. You can put
the dye bath in a bottle and save it for the next job of dying you want.
Or you can throw it down your sink drain, but be careful to place a
small piece of cheesecloth or old nylon stocking on top of the drain
so that pieces of wool won't clog it.

LARGE QUANTITY DYING–
RAINBOW METHOD

When you are dying fleece in large quantities, you can either use
one color as above, or you can use the rainbow method which Laurel
Scheeler, a spinner friend, taught me. This method produces a variety
of colors from one dye bath. When Laurel first showed me how to do
this, we dyed four fleeces in thirty-six hours. The virtue of this
method is that you get a surprise in every bath and there is never a
failure. Some fleece comes out darker, some lighter, and you may
get different colors than the ones you expected, but you never fail.

Spread your unwashed fleece (which will be greasy because it
still has the lanolin in it) out on a sheet. Pull out a chunk, the size of
a football.

Fill a big pot one quarter full of cool water. Add half a cup of
white vinegar, 1/8 cup Glauber salts (available at a photo supply store)
and three squirts of dish detergent. Stir. Add the fleece and poke it
down with a wooden stick which you can keep for future dying jobs
or discard. Never use a kitchen utensil. The fleece will soak up water
like a sponge and you should end up with just enough fleece so that
no water floats on top of the fleece.

Next, mentally divide the fleece in half. On each side sprinkle
a different color powdered RIT dye. Here are some possibilities:

Primary colors such as red & yellow, red & blue, blue & yellow; secondary colors such as purple & orange, green & orange, green & purple; primary & secondary colors such as orange & blue, purple & red, red & green. You can also try three or more colors although the fleece can get muddy. But what is wrong with mud colored hair?

Turn the flame on under the pot to simmer and leave for half an hour. After the water begins to boil gently, you will notice small volcanos coming up through the fleece. Where the volcanos are, you will get a blending of colors. If the colors are intense enough for you, take the fleece out immediately. If not, raise the heat gradually until you get the colors you want and then take the fleece out. Empty the hot dye bath into a sink or a pail. Please don't dump the dye bath on the earth. If you use your kitchen sink as a drain, put nylon or cheesecloth over the drain opening to catch loose strands.

Rinse the fleece out with warm water at your sink, gradually changing to cold water. When the water runs clear, you should press out the excess water. Place the fleece on an old towel or piece of cloth. You will find it has many colors; if you used red and yellow, for example, the color will range from bright red to pale pink, to brilliant orange and all shades of yellow and gold.

To dry the fleece, suspend a towel, hammock fashion, from two clothes lines or spread it out on a bush, Indian fashion. The important thing is to get the air circulating around it. If you have to lay it flat, be sure to keep turning it so that it doesn't mold.

When the fleece is dry, store it in a paper bag. You should have enough fleece for an entire family of dolls.

VEGETABLE DYING

Vegetable or natural dying is an extremely rewarding way to obtain color for wool. The dyes come from various plants that can be found in your own backyard, a nearby park or the woods. There are several excellent books available which give complete instructions and recipes:

Natural Dyes and Home Dying by Rita J. Adrosko. This book includes a history of natural dying in America.

Vegetable Dying by Alma Lesch. This book has a lot of recipes and includes a color chart.

These books may be ordered from Textile Resources, 3763 Durango Avenue, Los Angeles, California 90034.

Attaching Hair

When you find a hair-do that fits, secure it with straight pins. Please count the pins you put in so that you will know how many to take out (especially important if you are making the doll for a child). After you have pinned the hair in place, take a needle and thread that matches the hair and sew a running stitch around the whole head. Every half inch or so, make several very small stitches to make sure everything is secure. Remove the pins and pull on the hair gently to make sure it is fastened securely.

You can make a "wig" out of spun yarn by cutting three hanks of eight strands each, braiding them, wrapping the braid around the doll's head and sewing it down.

On the following two pages are examples of the five types of dolls for which I give instructions and patterns: A Very Simple Doll, The Dancing Doll, A Head Pillow, Lovely Ladies and Winged Women. Notice how I have varied these basic shapes with applique, painting and hair-dos.

5

A Very Simple Doll

This is a basic shape which is easy to construct since there are only two pieces, a front and back. However, the number of different dolls which can be made from this pattern is endless once you begin to use your imagination. The doll can be painted with as simple or as elaborate costume as you wish. And you can add embroidered features--clothing, jewelry, hats, pockets, buttons, etc. Enjoy making this doll. Don't be afraid to change things or alter the size of her face or hands. Do whatever you want to make her your own. A small change can make a big difference.

Finished size 10" high

See Chapter 3 for general instructions on proceeding from pattern to doll and for instructions on enlarging patterns.

Materials needed

heavy paper to make pattern
1/3 to 1/2 yard unbleached muslin
technical fountain pen
black India ink
textile paints
brushes
fiberfill stuffing
yarn or fleece for hair

Optional materials

embroidery thread
felt or fabric scraps for appliqued
or embroidered facial features

Note: If you decide to use applique or embroidery, it must be done while the pieces of cloth are still flat.

Instructions

Enlarge pattern on heavy paper.

Pin and cut two pieces of unbleached muslin.

Pin right sides of fabric together. Sew back piece to front piece, leaving 2" opening at bottom.

Clip seams.

Turn and stuff with fiberfill.

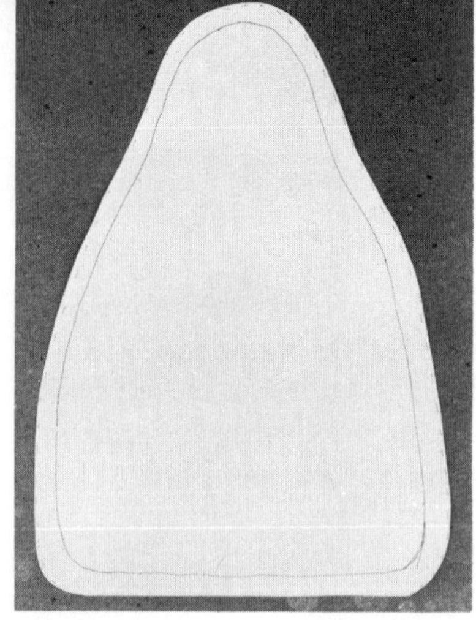

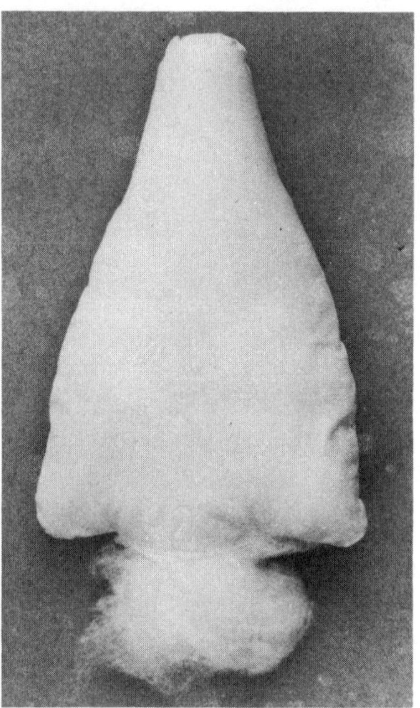

Handsew opening closed.

Using a technical fountain pen, draw the face. You may want to practice first, using a scrap of muslin.

Draw the outline of the clothing on the doll.

Decide whether you want a pattern on this clothing, such as tiny hearts or stars. If so, outline these with your pen.

Paint the face and body.

Apply hair. See page 47.

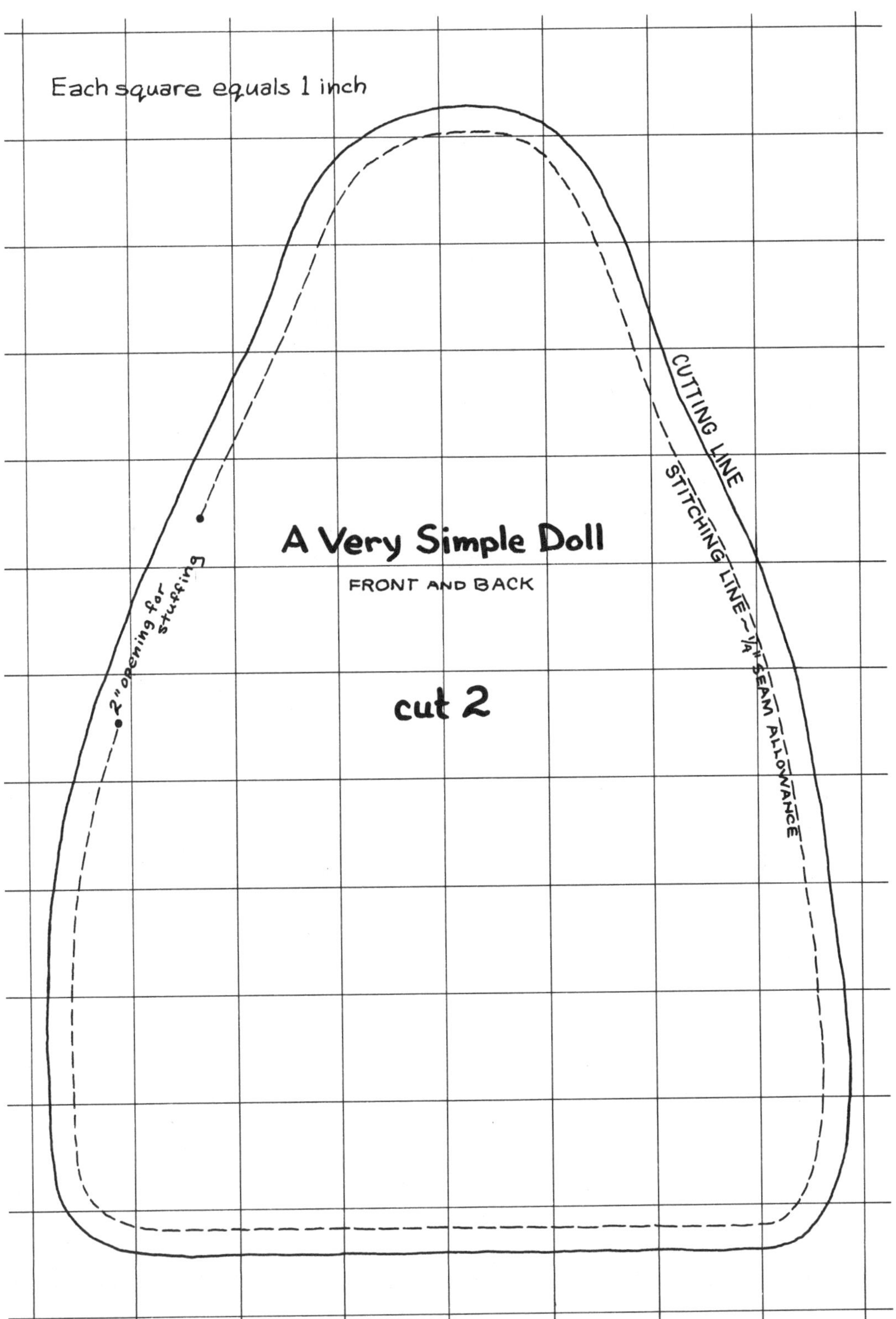

Each square equals 1 inch
A Very Simple Doll
FRONT AND BACK
cut 2
2" opening for stuffing
CUTTING LINE
STITCHING LINE ~ 1/4" SEAM ALLOWANCE

Back View of A Very Simple Doll

6
The Dancing Doll

This is a variation on A Very Simple Doll. It also has two pieces of fabric joined together, but the arms and legs have been differentiated from the body in order to provide more movement and more possible detail. This doll, like A Very Simple Doll, has a painted face and body.

Finished size: 10" high

See Chapter 3 for general instructions on proceeding from pattern to doll and for instructions on enlarging patterns.

Materials needed

heavy paper to make pattern
1/3 to 1/2 yard unbleached muslin
technical fountain pen
black India ink
textile paints
brushes
fiberfill stuffing
yarn or fleece for hair

Optional materials

embroidery thread
felt and fabric scraps for appliqued or embroidered facial features

Note: If you decide to use applique or embroidery, this work must be done while the pieces of cloth are still flat.

Instructions

Enlarge pattern on heavy paper.

Pin and cut two pieces from muslin.

Pin right sides together and then sew front to back, leaving a 2" opening at side.

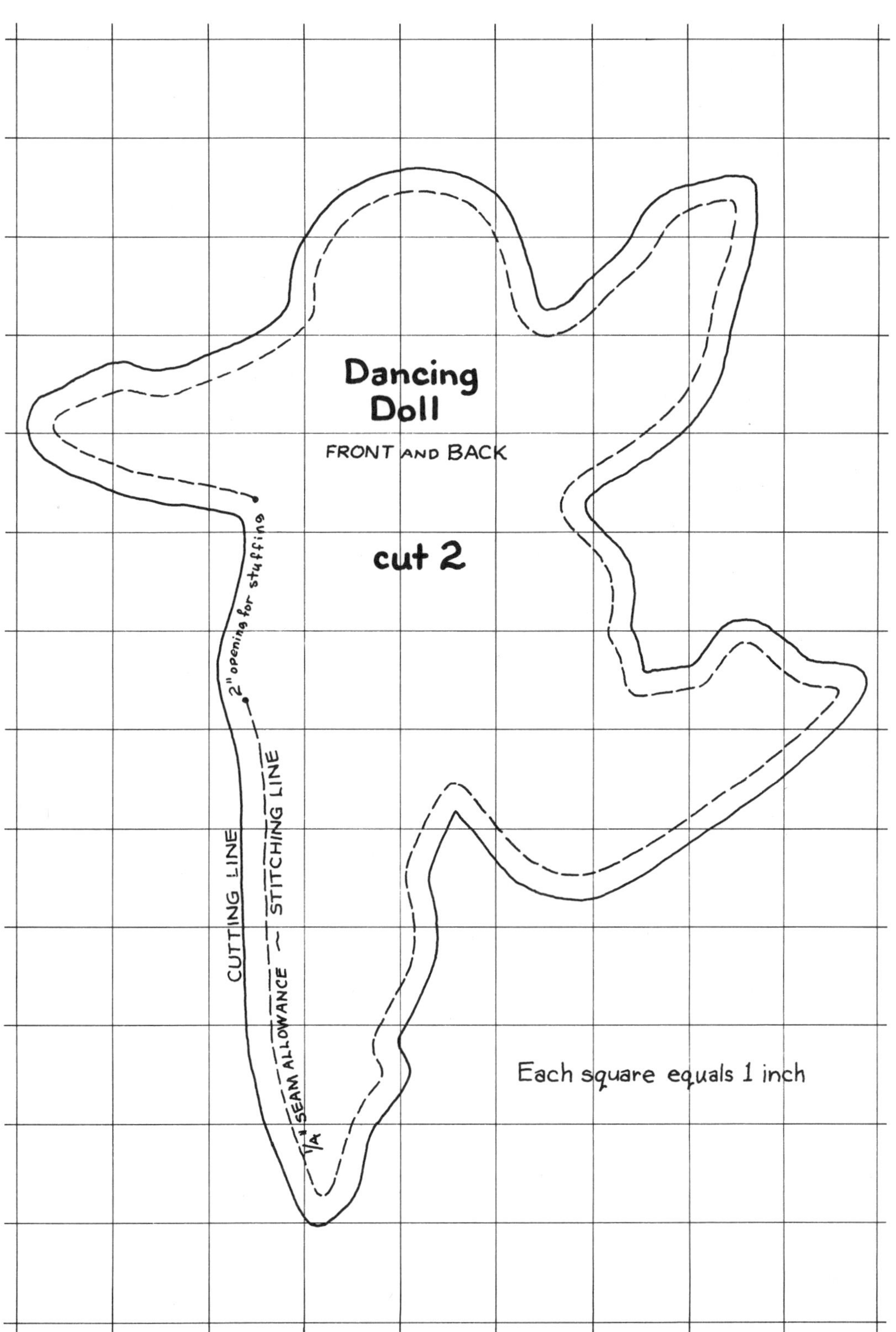

Dancing
Doll
FRONT AND BACK
cut 2
2" opening for stuffing
CUTTING LINE
STITCHING LINE
1/4" SEAM ALLOWANCE
Each square equals 1 inch

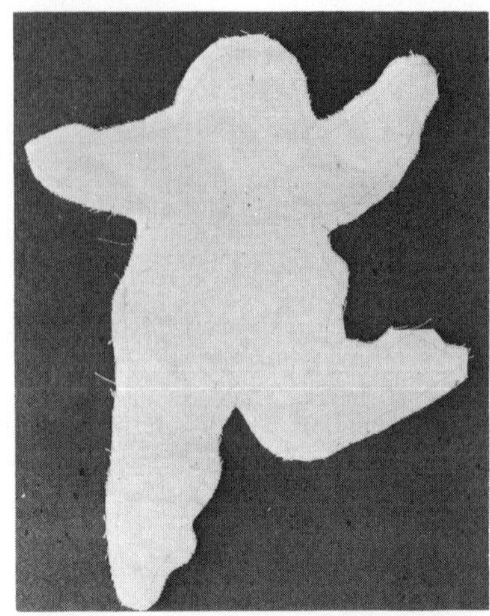

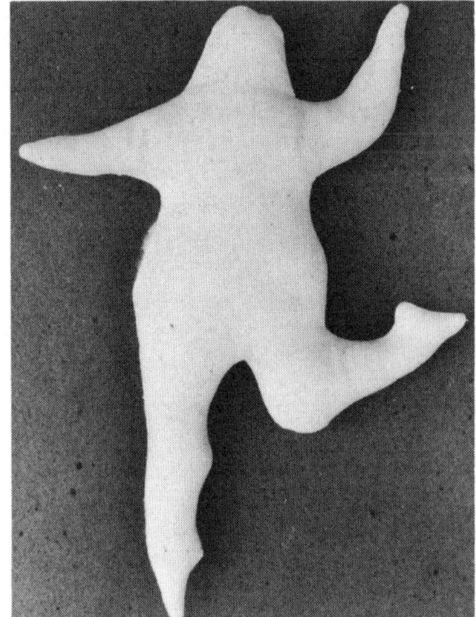

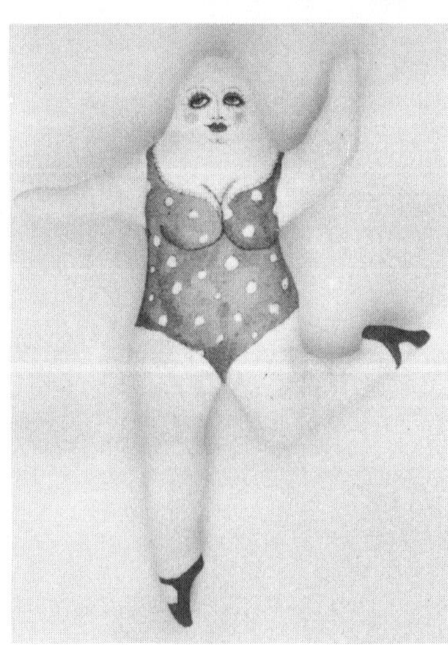

Clip and trim seams.

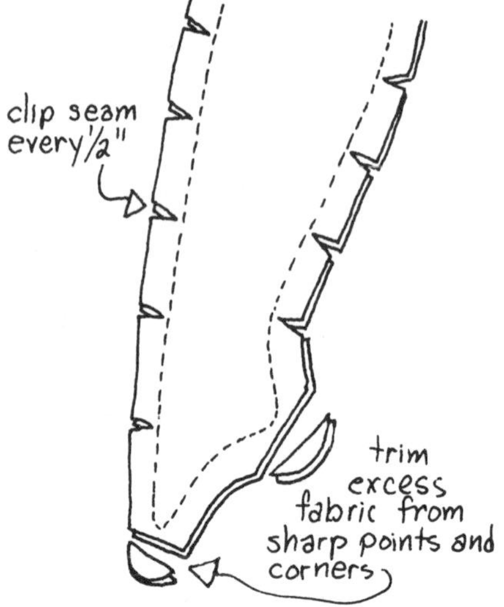

Turn and stuff with fiberfill.

Hand sew opening closed.

Draw the face and clothing on body with technical fountain pen. Use photos as guide.

Paint in the features and clothing.

Apply hair. See page 47.

Back View of The Dancing Doll

7

A Head Pillow

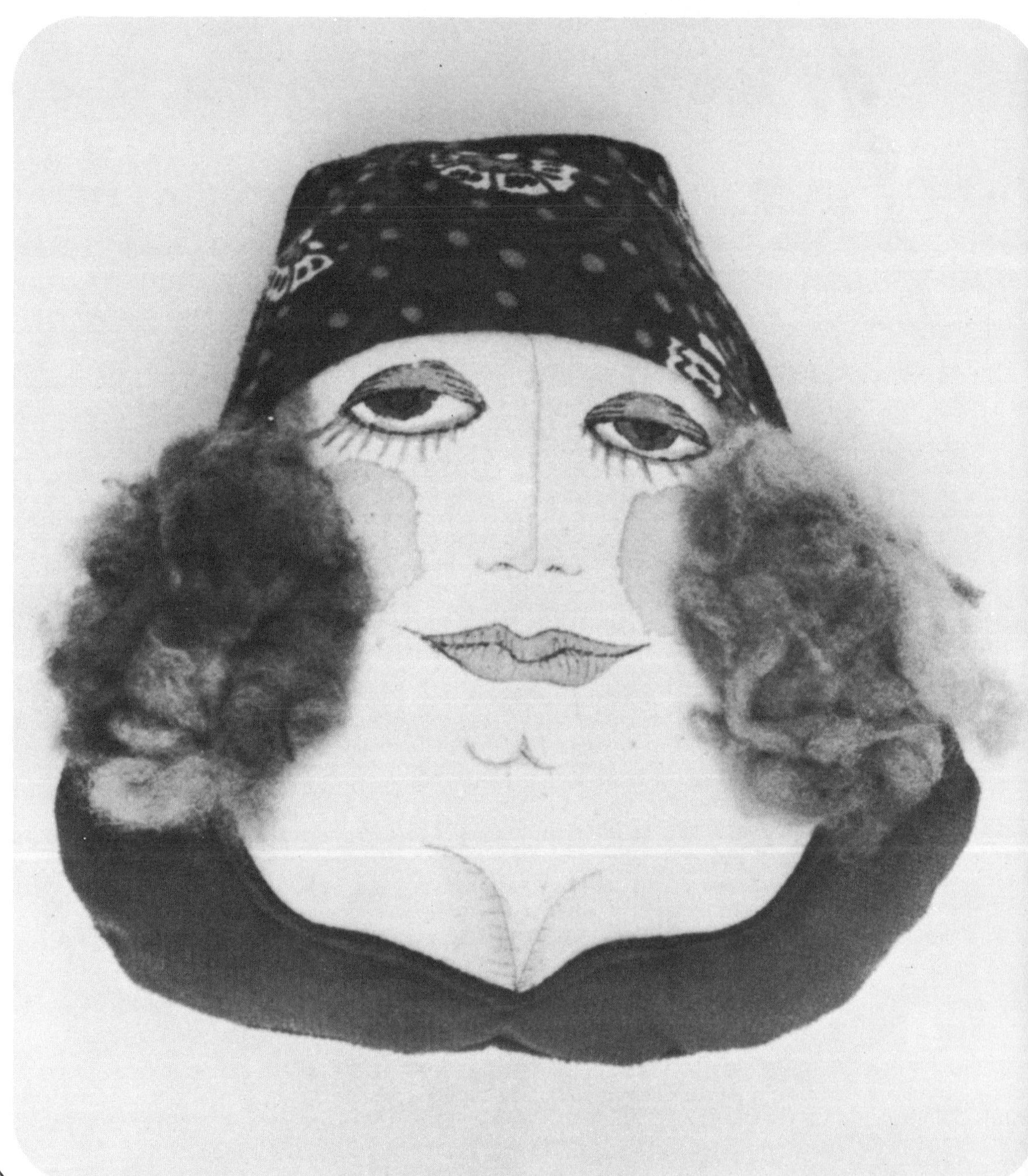

Head Pillows are great fun. On a very basic shape, I add an appliqued dress, hair, and usually a bandanna or hat. The features of these head pillows are larger than my other dolls' so that painting the face is a lot like putting make up on. There is also more room for using found objects, such as jewelry, pieces of necklines from real dresses such as old fancy cocktail dresses, spaghetti straps, or lace from strips. I once made a doll which showed the adjustment part of a bra strap. In other words, anything that fits can go on this doll.

Finished size 7" high

See Chapter 3 for general instructions on proceeding from pattern to doll and the instructions on transferring patterns.

Materials needed

heavy paper to make pattern
1/3 yard fabric for dress and pillow back
12" square unbleached muslin
technical fountain pen
black India ink
textile paints
brushes
fiberfill stuffing
yarn or fleece for hair
lace, ribbons and rickrack, buttons, beads, and so on for dress trim

Optional materials

embroidery thread
felt or fabric scraps for appliqued or embroidered facial features

Note: If you decide to use applique or embroidery, this work must be done while the pieces of cloth are still flat.

Instructions

Transfer pattern to heavy paper.

Pin and cut one front of muslin.

Using a technical fountain pen, draw the facial features on muslin front. Either use photograph as a guide, or use your own imagination. Or you can embroider or applique the face; it's up to you.

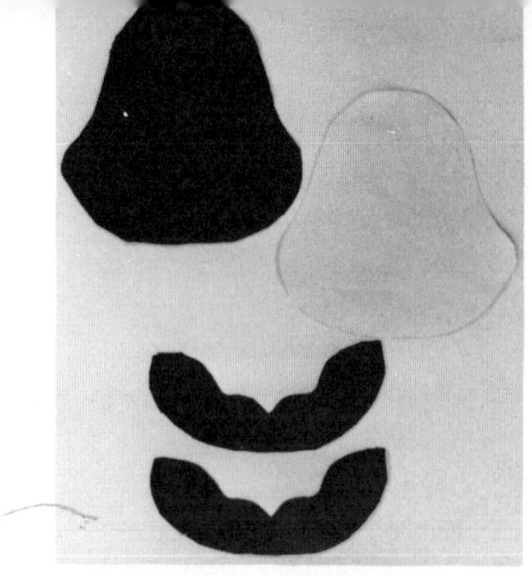

Pin and cut one dress back and two dress fronts.

With right sides together, pin dress front pieces along neck line. Sew the two dress fronts together.

Clip seam. Turn and press.

Pin dress front to right side of muslin front along neckline. Then top stitch. Add any trims you want: lace, ribbons, buttons, etc., to dress front.

With rights sides together, pin back to front, making sure dress front is attached along bottom seam. Sew, leaving 2" opening on side or top of head.

Clip seam. Turn and press.

Stuff with fiberfill.

Handsew the opening closed.

Apply hair. See page 47.

Paint the face, keeping the color scheme of your doll's dress in mind.

Instructions for optional bandanna

Fold 15" square of fabric into a triangle, right sides together.

Pin and stitch sides together, leaving a 2" opening.

Clip corners and turn right sides out.

Tuck in edges of opening and press.

Top stitch sewn edges close to edge. Opening will be sewn closed when done.

Tie bandanna on head of doll. Tack down knot in back and on either side of face, to hold it in place.

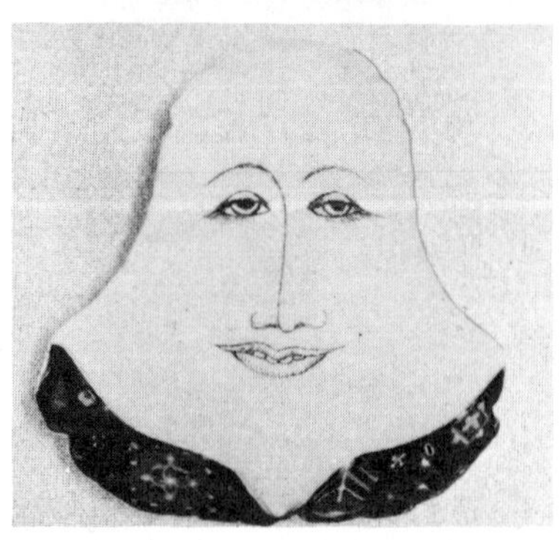

62

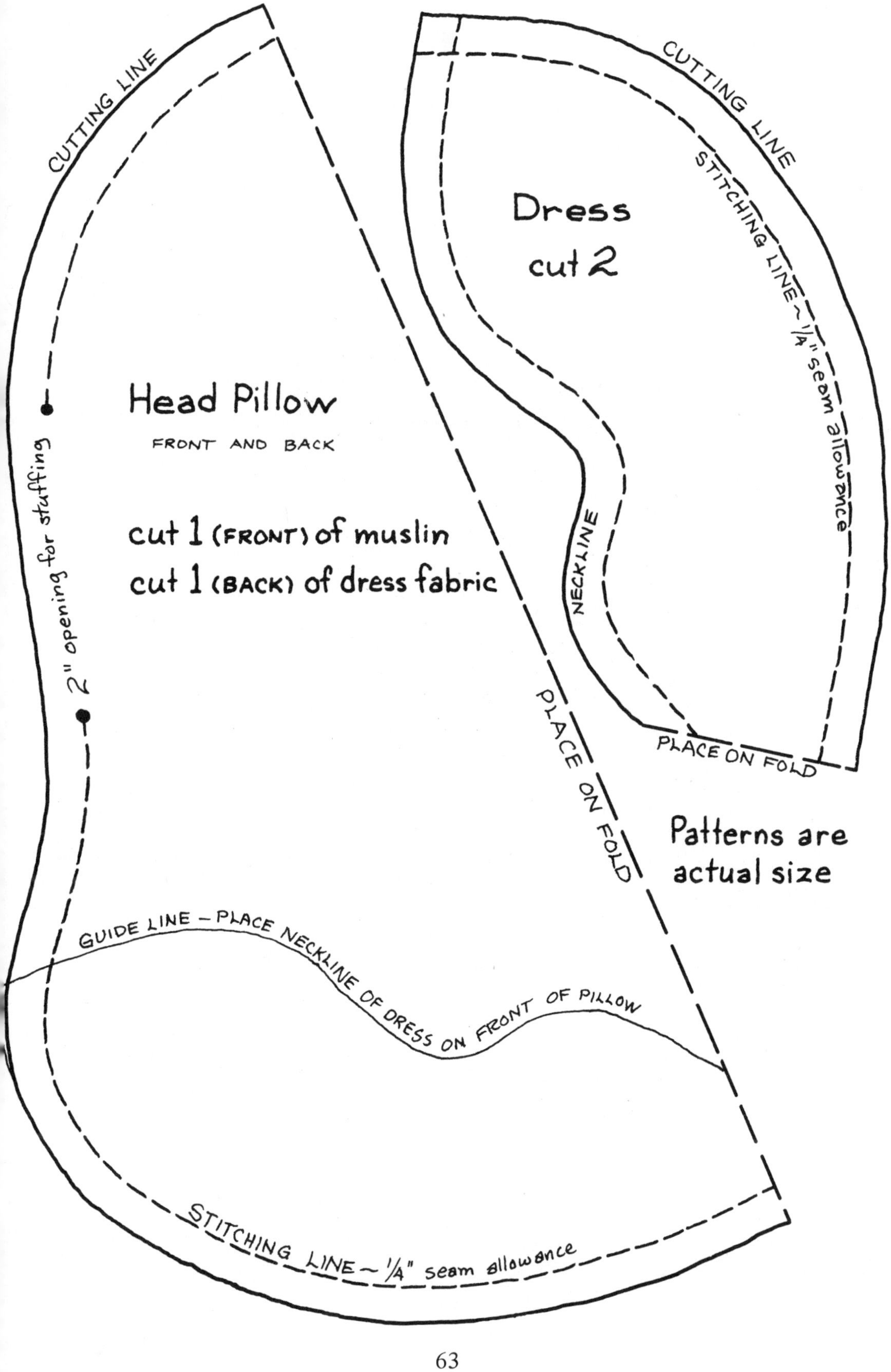

CUTTING LINE
CUTTING LINE
STITCHING LINE ~ 1/4" seam allowance
Dress
cut 2
Head Pillow
FRONT AND BACK
cut 1 (FRONT) of muslin
cut 1 (BACK) of dress fabric
2" opening for stuffing
NECKLINE
PLACE ON FOLD
PLACE ON FOLD
PLACE ON FOLD
Patterns are
actual size
GUIDE LINE — PLACE NECKLINE OF DRESS ON FRONT OF PILLOW
STITCHING LINE ~ 1/4" seam allowance

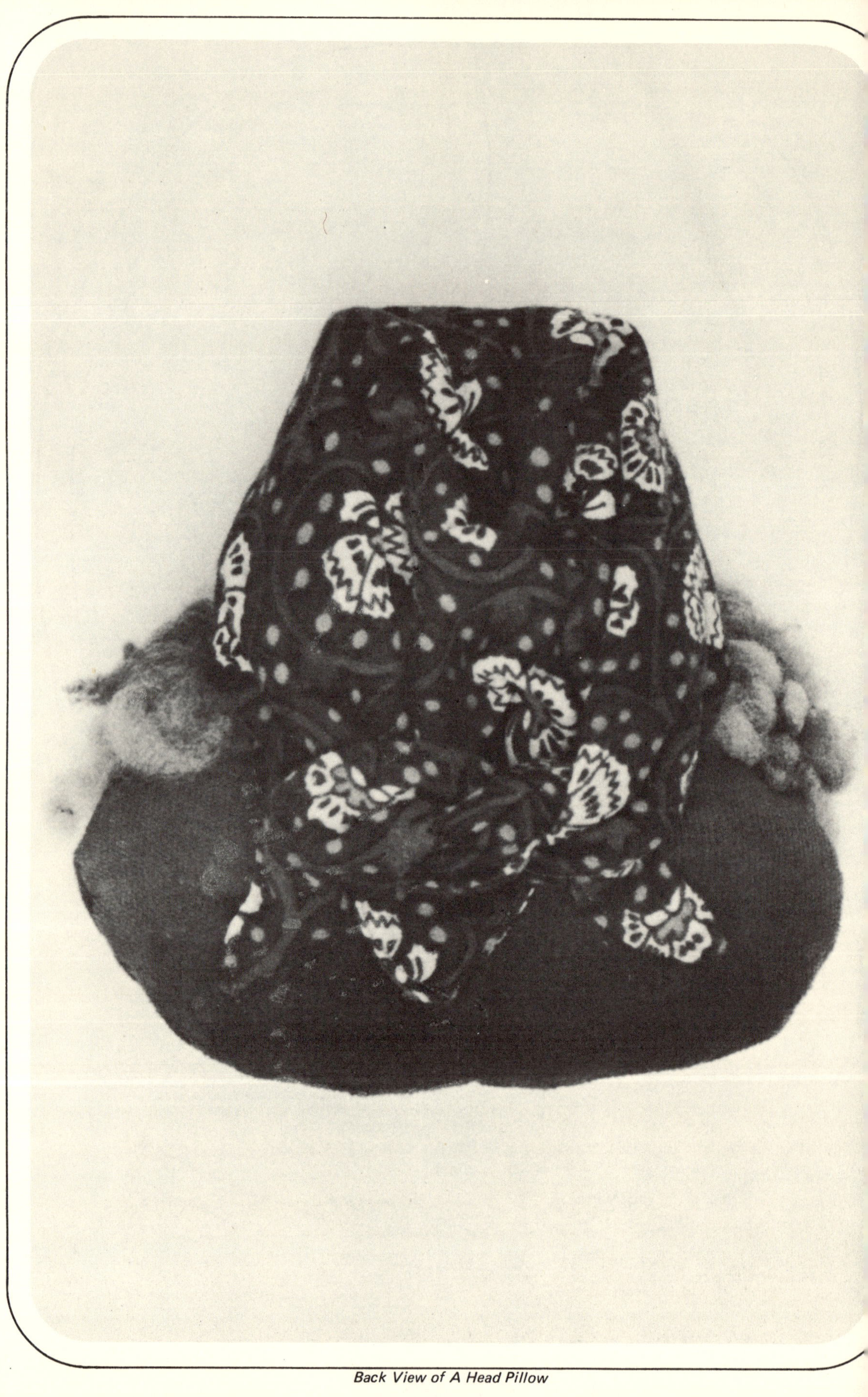

Back View of A Head Pillow

8

Winged Women

Winged Women are fun to play with--they come with a back pocket filled with a tiny gift or surprise. These surprises can be anything your heart desires, from a new automobile (a stuffed drawing of your favorite car) to a vacation in the Mediterranean (simply do a pillow map of your favorite resort). My Winged Women have had pillows of frogs, little angels, glasses of champagne, and dishes of fruit. Pocket items can add a nice twist to the idea your Winged Woman expresses.

Finished size 7" high

See Chapter 3 for general instructions on proceeding from pattern to doll and for instructions on transferring patterns.

Materials needed

heavy paper to make pattern
1/3 to 1/2 yard fabric for body and dress
scraps of unbleached muslin for face and pocket item
scraps of various fabrics for wings and pocket
lace, ribbon, buttons, beads, feathers, etc., for trims
technical fountain pen
black India ink
textile paints
fiberfill stuffing
yarn or fleece for hair

Instructions

Transfer patterns on heavy paper.

Pin and cut 2 body pieces from fabric.

Pin and cut face from muslin scrap. Draw features with pen on muslin, using photo as a guide if you like.

Place a small ball of fiberfill under the face and set on top of front

PLACE ON FOLD

Face ~ cut 1

TURN UNDER 1/4"

Pocket Item ~ cut 2

CUTTING LINE

CUTTING LINE

STITCHING LINE ~ 1/8" seam allowance

1" opening for stuffing

All Patterns are actual size

Winged Women

Body

FRONT AND BACK

cut 2

CUTTING LINE

STITCHING LINE ~ 1/8" seam allowance

Wing

cut 4
(2 PAIRS)

leave opening for stuffing

1" opening for turning

CUTTING LINE

Pocket

cut 2

PLACE ON FOLD

PLACE ON FOLD

STITCHING LINE ~ 1/4" seam allowance

CUTTING LINE

STITCHING LINE ~ 1/4" seam allowance

2" opening for stuffing

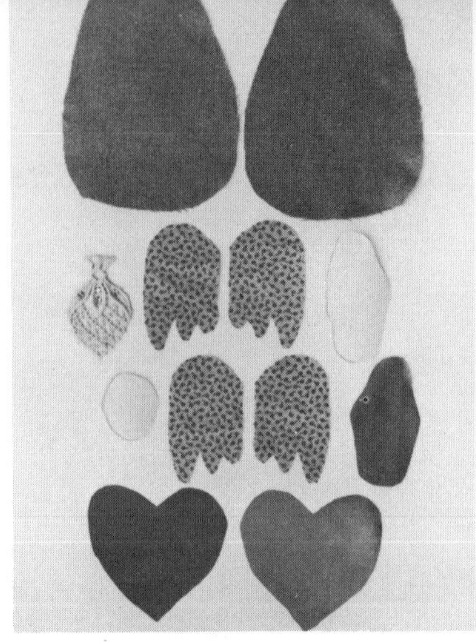

body piece. Pin, tucking raw edges under ¼" all around.

Top stitch as close to edge as possible. When stitching with machine, go very slowly so that you can control the turning.

After face is secured, quilt at corners of eyes, nose and mouth; this will add 3 dimension look to the face.

Lace Applique

Cut a motif from a piece of lace.

Locate and pin to body front. Top stitch in place.

Optional: If you would prefer hands instead of lace applique, see hand instructions in next chapter, "Lovely Ladies."

Pocket

Cut two pocket pieces from co-ordinated fabrics (outside and lining).

Pin with right sides together. Sew, leaving 1" opening. Clip and trim seams.

Turn to right side, tucking in raw edges and press.

Arrange pocket on body back. Pin and topstitch pocket to back. Be sure to leave top of pocket open.

Wings

Cut two pairs of wings from fabric scraps.

Pin with right sides together. Sew, leaving ends open.

Clip and trim seams. Turn inside out. Stuff with fiberfill.

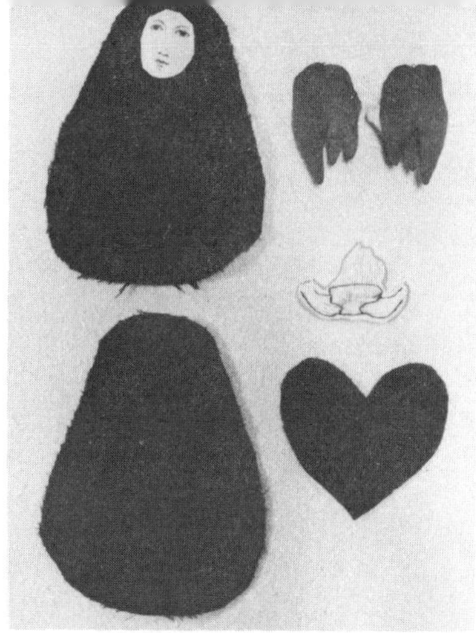

Body

Locate and pin wings to front of body.

Right sides together, pin front and back of body with wings sandwiched between. Stitch, leaving 2" opening at bottom.

Clip seams. Trim off excess wing material at seam.

Turn and stuff with fiberfill. Hand sew opening closed.

Apply hair. See page 47.

Crown

Cut a three pointed motif from a piece of lace.

Position on head and tack in place.

Pocket Item

Cut two pocket item pieces from muslin.

With pen, draw design on front piece.

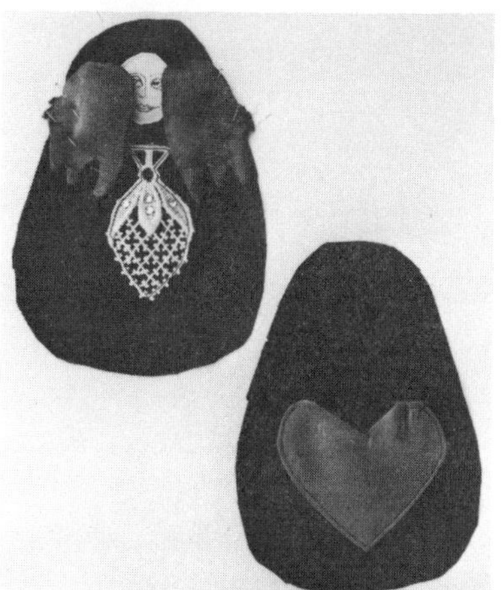

With right sides together, pin back and front pieces. Sew, leaving 1" opening.

Clip and trim seam. Turn inside out.

Stuff with fiberfill. Hand sew opening closed.

Paint facial features and pocket item.

Stuff pocket item into pocket.

Note: Stitch a loop of thread between doll and pocket item to prevent loss if the doll is to be sold.

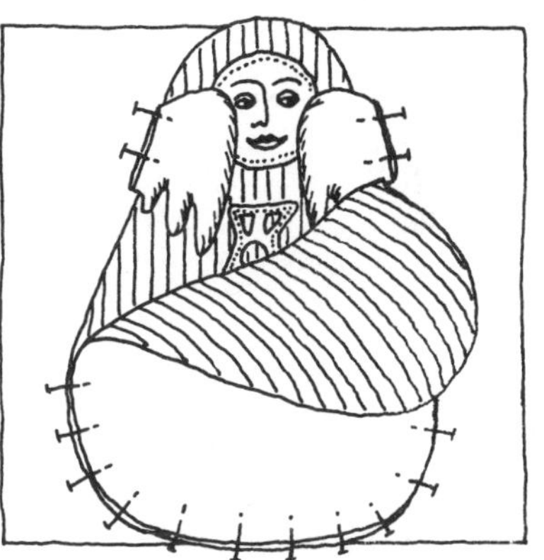

69

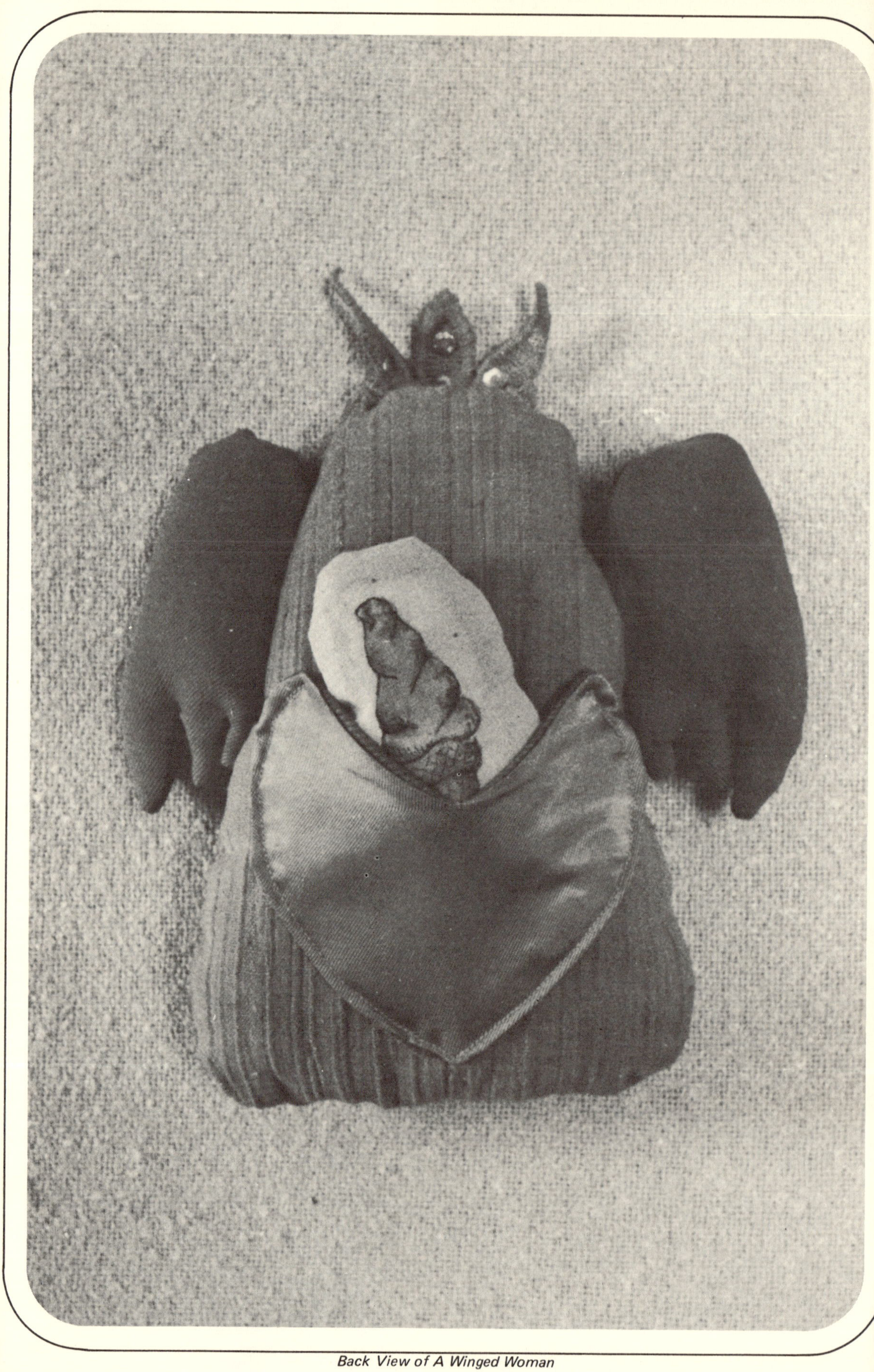

Back View of A Winged Woman

9
Lovely Ladies

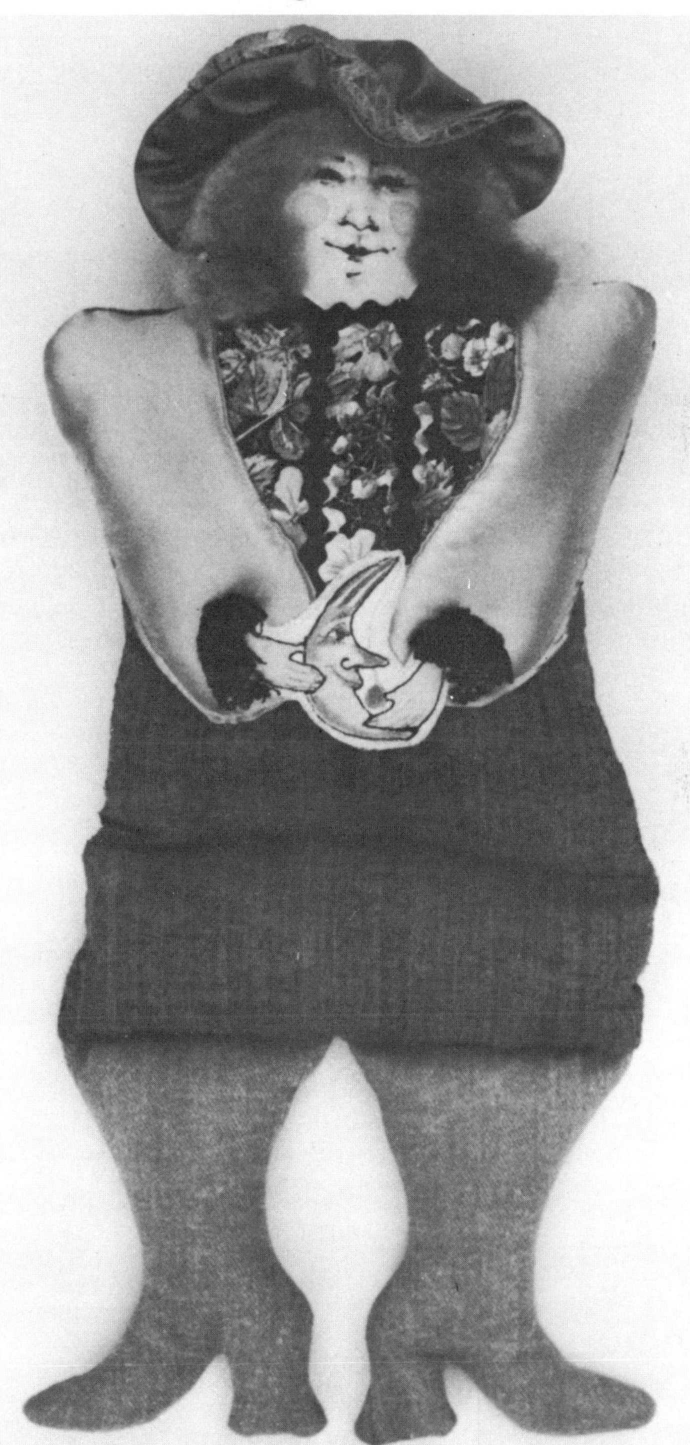

Lovely ladies are a very regal group; even when made with plain fabric, these dolls have a certain sophistication. I like to increase their appeal, however, with as much velvet, satin, brocade and lace as I can muster. What they are holding is part of their appeal. You will have to figure this out for the doll you make. I try to give them something a bit preposterous or silly to hold. I confess I love slapstick comedy. The vision of a satin doll seated on a red silk davenport holding a dripping chocolate sundae completely delights me.

Finished size 15-½" high

See Chapter 3 for general instructions on proceeding from pattern to doll and for instructions on enlarging patterns.

Materials needed

heavy paper to make pattern
1/3 to 1/2 yard fabric for body and dress of doll
scraps of unbleached muslin for face and hands
scraps of various fabrics for blouse, arms and boots; hat lace,
     rickrack, ribbons, beads, buttons, feathers and jewels for trims.
technical fountain pen
textile paints
brushes
fiberfill stuffing
yarn or fleece for hair

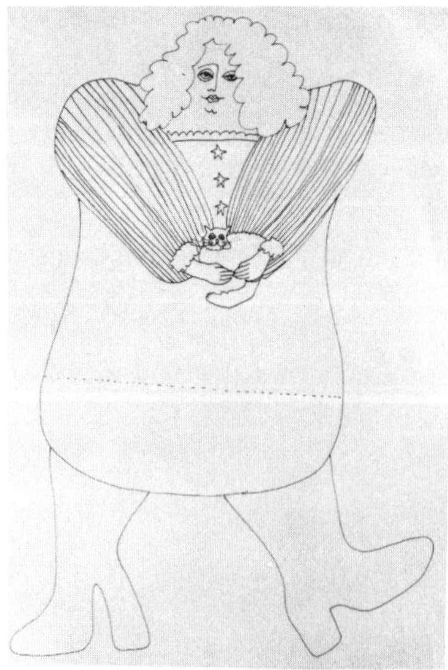

Instructions

Enlarge patterns on heavy paper.

Pin and cut two body pieces from fabric.

Face

Cut face from muslin scrap. Draw features with pen on muslin, using photo as guide if you wish.

Place a small ball of fiberfill under face and set on top of body piece. Pin, tucking raw edges under ¼" all around.

Topstitch as close to edge as possible. When stitching with machine,

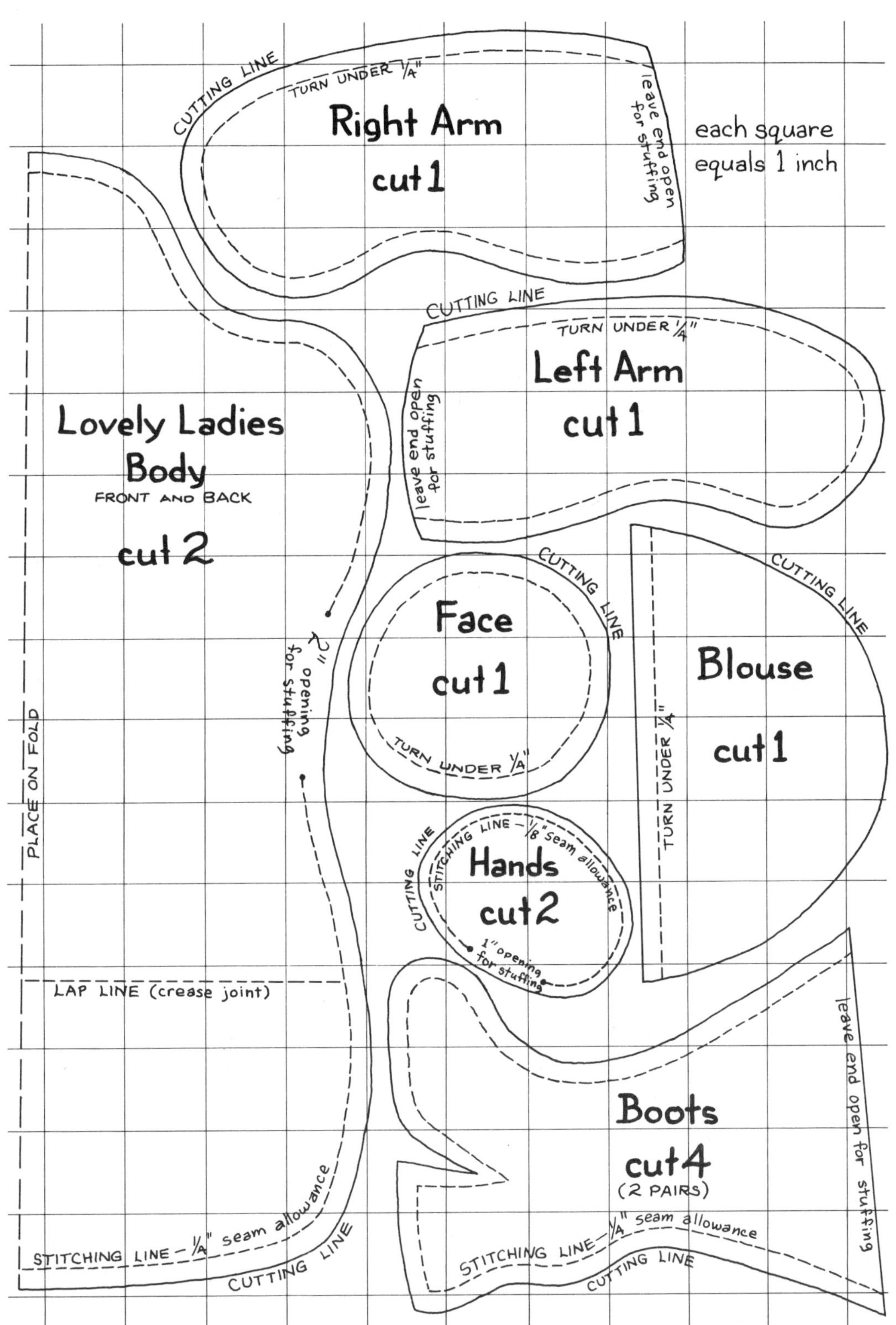

CUTTING LINE
TURN UNDER ¼"
Right Arm
cut 1
leave end open for stuffing
each square equals 1 inch
CUTTING LINE
TURN UNDER ¼"
Left Arm
cut 1
leave end open for stuffing
Lovely Ladies Body
FRONT AND BACK
cut 2
PLACE ON FOLD
LAP LINE (crease joint)
2" opening for stuffing
CUTTING LINE
Face
cut 1
TURN UNDER ¼"
CUTTING LINE
Blouse
cut 1
TURN UNDER ¼"
CUTTING LINE
STITCHING LINE — ⅛" seam allowance
Hands
cut 2
1" opening for stuffing
Boots
cut 4
(2 PAIRS)
leave end open for stuffing
STITCHING LINE — ¼" seam allowance
CUTTING LINE
STITCHING LINE — ¼" seam allowance
CUTTING LINE

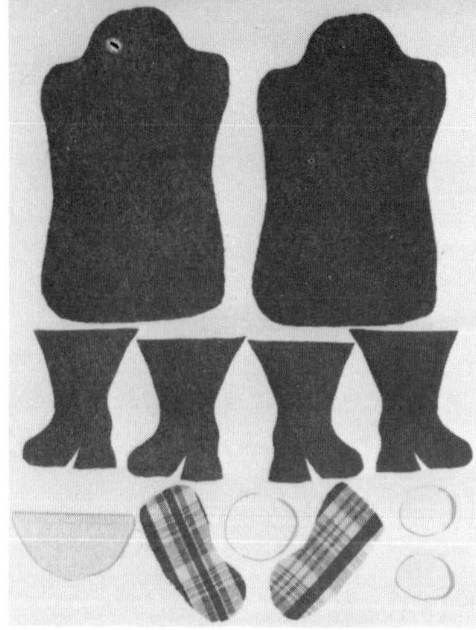

go very slowly so that you can control the turning.

After face is secured, quilt at corners of eyes, nose and mouth to add a third dimension.

Blouse
Cut blouse from coordinating fabric.

Press under ¼" on top edge. Pin onto right side of body front, just below the face. Topstitch.

Add lace or ribbon, buttons, beads, etc., as trims. Keep in mind that the lace trim at the top of the blouse helps hide the applique seam at the base of the doll's face. This gives the doll a more realistic look.

Arms/Sleeves
The arms and sleeves are all one piece. Use a coordinating fabric and cut one right arm and one left arm.

Press under ¼" around edge, excluding top of shoulder.

Place on right side of body front. Pin and topstitch, leaving shoulders open. Fabric should extend ½" beyond shoulder.

Hands
Cut two hand pieces from muslin scrap.

Using pen, draw hand details on top hand piece, using photo as guide if you like. Hands may be clasped or holding something.

With right sides together, pin front and back of hands. Sew, leaving 1" opening.

74

Clip seam and turn.

Stuff very lightly with fiberfill. Turn in raw edges and handsew opening closed.

To quilt, stitch around outline of hands and object being held.

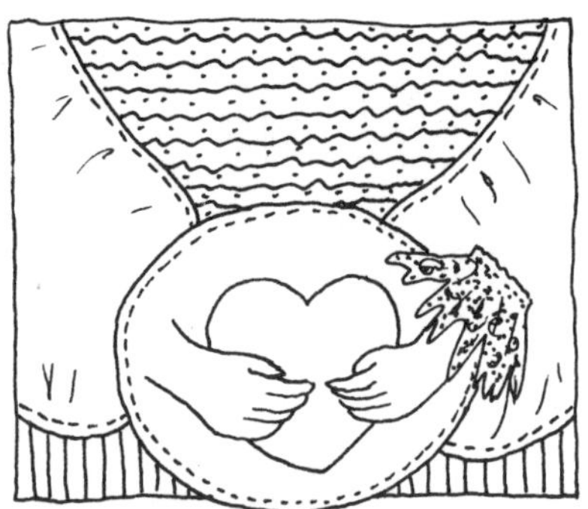

Place hands over wrist end of sleeves. Pin and topstitch through sleeves, blouse and body front.

Gather a small piece of lace and sew to body at the point the wrists and sleeves meet.

Stuff arm very lightly with small amounts of fiberfill, leaving room for joining seam at top.

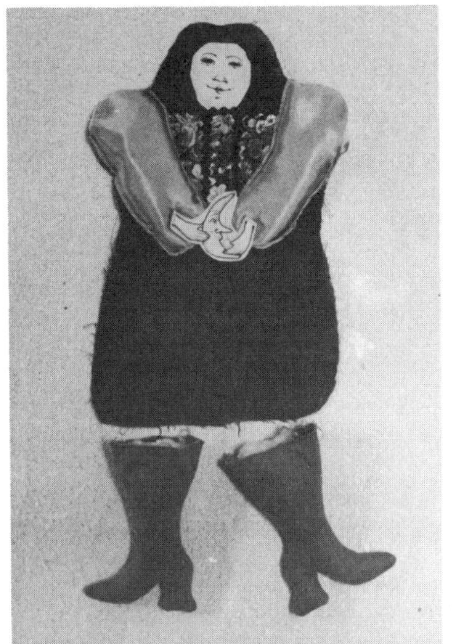

Boots

Fold boot fabric, right sides together. Cut two pairs of boots.

With right sides together, pin back and front. Sew, leaving tops open.

Clip seams. Trim heel corners and make a notch where heel meets instep.

Turn and stuff with fiberfill, leaving ½" at top for joining seam. Place boots on front of doll and pin.

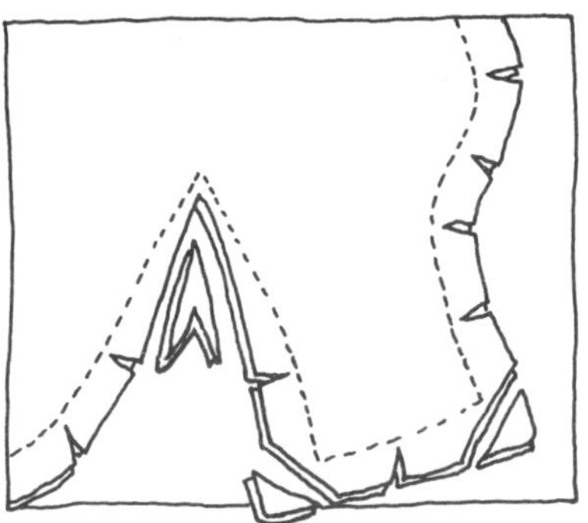

Body

With right sides together, pin front and back of body with boots sandwiched between. Stitch, leaving 2" opening at the side between arm and lap line.

Clip seam and trim excess material at shoulders and boots.

Turn and stuff bottom to lap line.

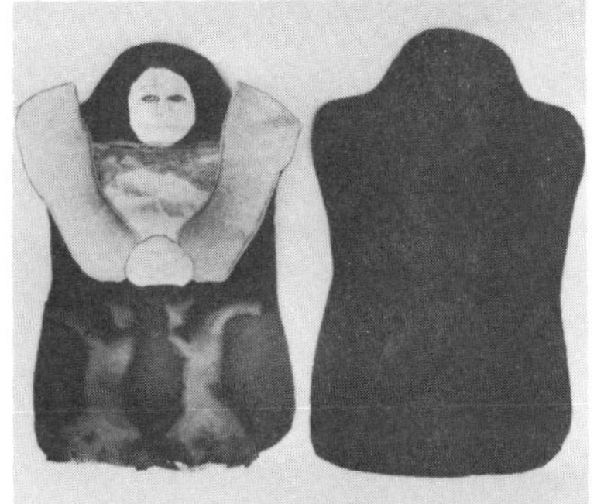

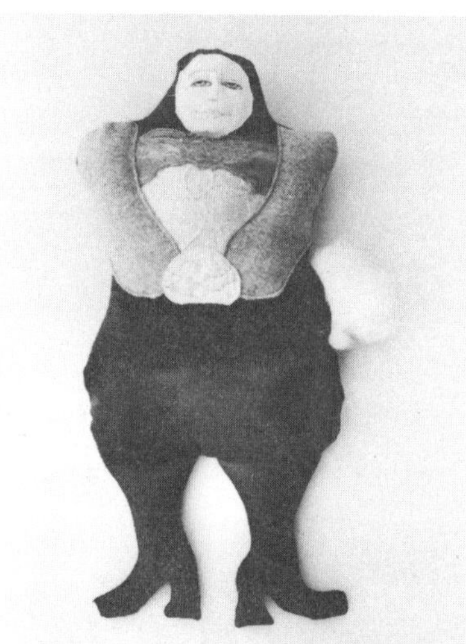

With matching thread, machine stitch a seam along the lap line across doll through both back and front of body.

Finish stuffing. Handsew opening closed.

Apply hair. See page 47.

Paint facial features and object being held.

Instructions for Optional Hat

Cut two 7" circles from coordinating fabrics.

Pin with right sides together. Sew, leaving 2" opening.

Clip seam and turn inside out.

Tuck in raw edges of opening and press. Topstitch close to edge.

By hand, sew a running stitch 1" from edge. Place on doll and pull thread to gather, fitting to doll's head. Secure thread.

Attach hat to head.

Hatband can be lace or a tube of fabric. Handsew band over gathering stitches, turning under ends for a neat finish.

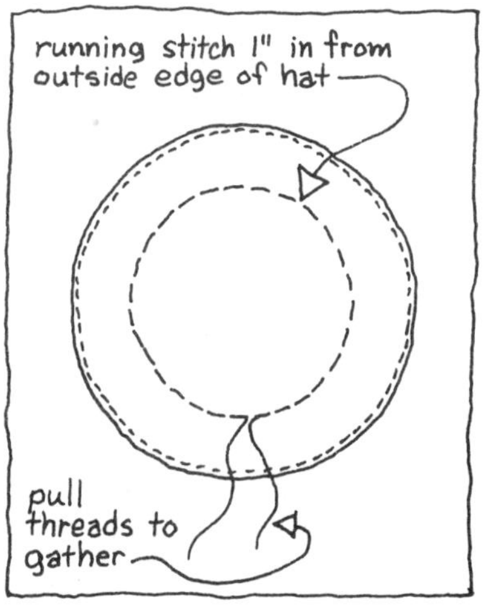

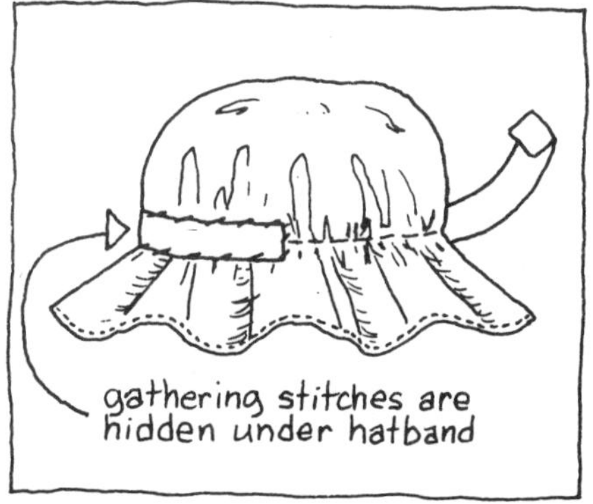

Back View of A Lovely Lady

10

Special Dolls

The photographs on the following pages show different things I've done with the techniques used in the simple dolls I have shown you. Some emphasize painting, others trapunto and quilting, others applique. I am sure new ideas for dolls will come to you as you continue to build on the skills you have acquired. An important note for your own creativity: these "soft" techniques can be combined with other arts and crafts, such as weaving or wood carving, thus making a doll that is uniquely yours.

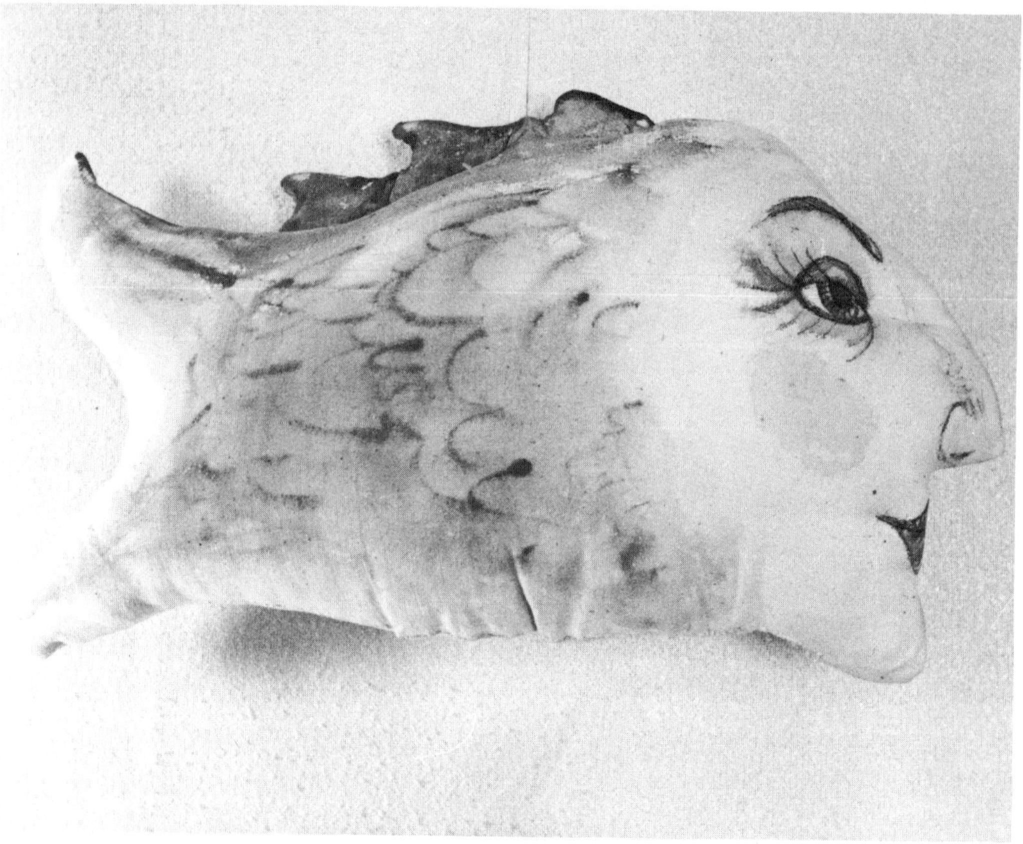

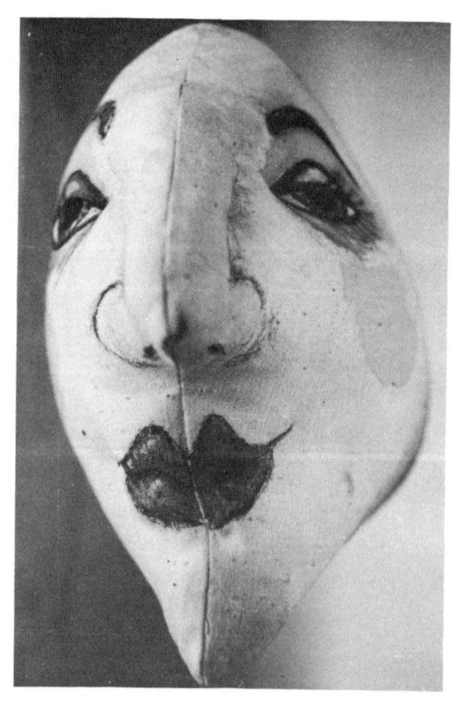

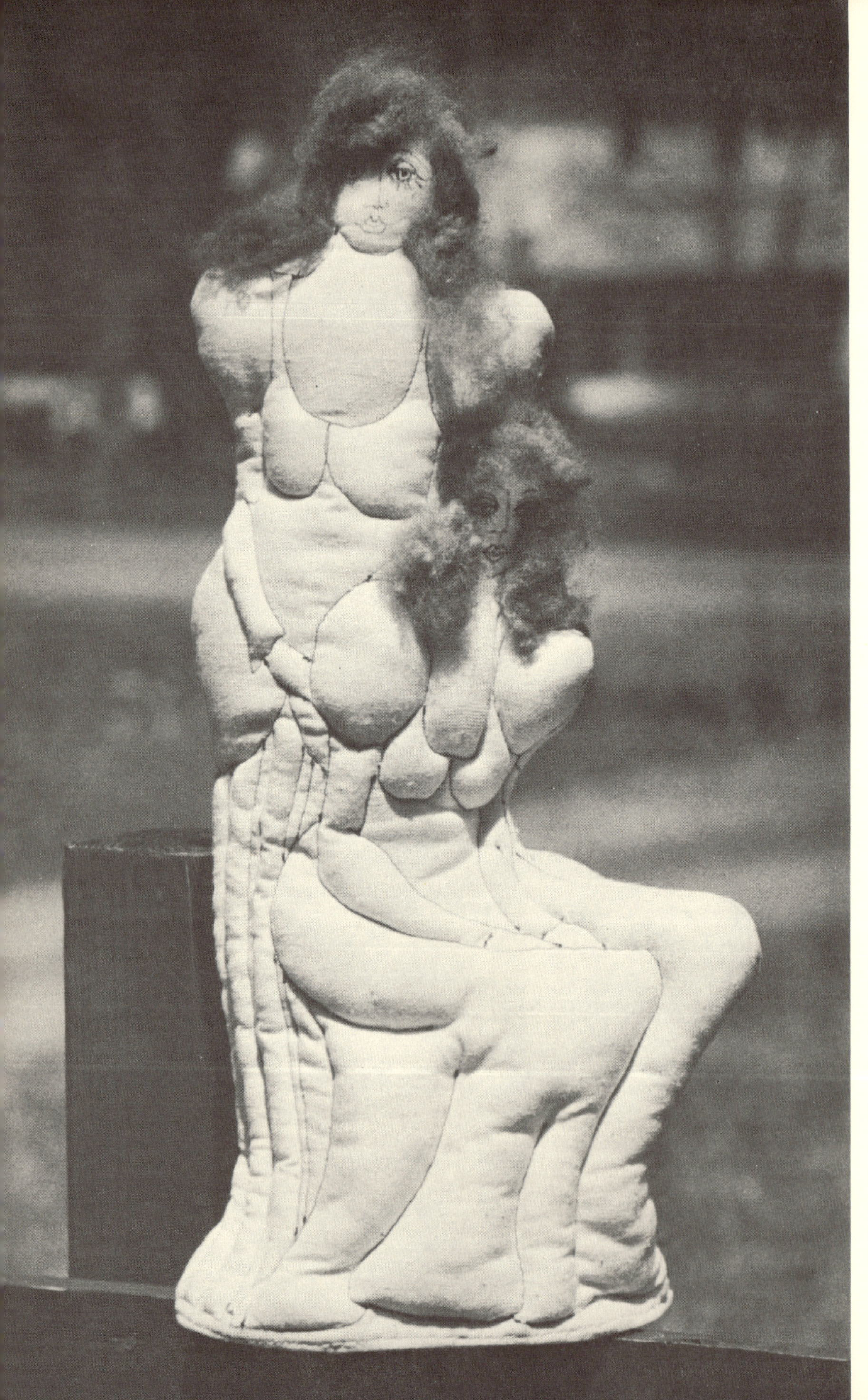

11

Marketing

I don't have any hard and fast rules about marketing. I feel a good doll will sell itself if given half a chance.

I began my career selling dolls when I produced a doll who looked as though she ran a brothel, someone who saw the real underside of life but had enough gusto to hold her own. Thinking she was too hideous for anyone to see, I hid her away in a shady corner of the house. But some friends saw her and liked her. They insisted I enter her in a local Christmas fair. I was nervous but made a few more dolls and took them all to the fair. I came home with

$53 and felt great. Encouraged, I entered another fair and made $82. At the next Christmas fair, I came home with $390. The point I am making is that you should not be afraid to show your work.

Once you have entered your dolls in a fair, please observe people's reactions. See what types of dolls people will buy and don't be afraid to adapt your dolls to make maximum sales.

Places to Exhibit

The best place to begin is a local crafts sale. There are two kinds, those open to anyone and those with entries selected by jurors. For the open sales, contact the persons in charge or ask a craftsperson who plans to exhibit for details on entering. At the juried sales, you will have to submit dolls or slides to jurors who will make their decision on the basis of quality and originality. If you submit slides, make sure they are good slides with clear images and unobtrusive backgrounds. If you aren't sure of your skills as a photographer, get a professional to do the work for you. As for the background for your dolls, use an ironed piece of plain fabric.

If you live in an area which doesn't have crafts sales, you will have to create places to show your work. Some places will just exhibit for you. Others will exhibit and sell for you.

Banks, museums, restaurants, art galleries, theater lobbies and department store windows will exhibit dolls for you if you ask them to. Be brave. It's fun for people to see a doll show. If it seems overwhelming to do a show all by yourself, get a friend to share it with you.

Toy stores, antique stores, fabric stores and furniture stores may exhibit and sell your work for you. Don't hesitate to approach the managers asking them to handle your dolls on a consignment basis. Offer them 30% of the selling price, payable to you once the doll is sold.

The professional guilds sometimes have annual group shows where you can exhibit your work. And, of course, working with others can be a wonderful source of inspiration. I belong to the Textile Arts Guild in Ithaca, New York, which meets once a month so that we can share projects by showing slides of our current work. In addition, we rent slide kits from the American Art Council in New York City so that we can see what other people are doing.

Displaying Your Dolls

If you are exhibiting at a sale where you can design your own booth or table, decide first whether you want to hang your dolls or show them sitting or standing on a shelf. You should keep your design flexible so that it can fit in a variety of spaces—the amount of space you can get at a fair varies. You should also make your design portable so that you can put it in your car to take to fairs.

The dolls I have described in this book are all suitable for shelf display. I like to see multi-level displays, done simply with cardboard boxes draped with fabric. But cardboard will not stand up to weather. For more permanent structures, you can use plywood and cinder blocks or make your own plywood boxes to be painted whatever colors you wish.

Don't forget to provide for storage space beneath the display area. This is the reason I like boxes. You can store things under them. You can also use boxes set on their sides as nice display places and set your dolls into little tableaus.

If you are exhibiting at a fair, you should find out if you can display the dolls in one group or whether the directors reserve the right to arrange the dolls wherever they please. I have mixed feelings on the matter. On the one hand, the dolls sitting together in one space create a dramatic impact. On the other hand, since dolls are magnetic, they create attention wherever they are, in the midst of weavings, pottery, whatever. If you are able to get an area put aside solely for your dolls with the overflow put in strategic spots around the fair, I think you have the best of both worlds.

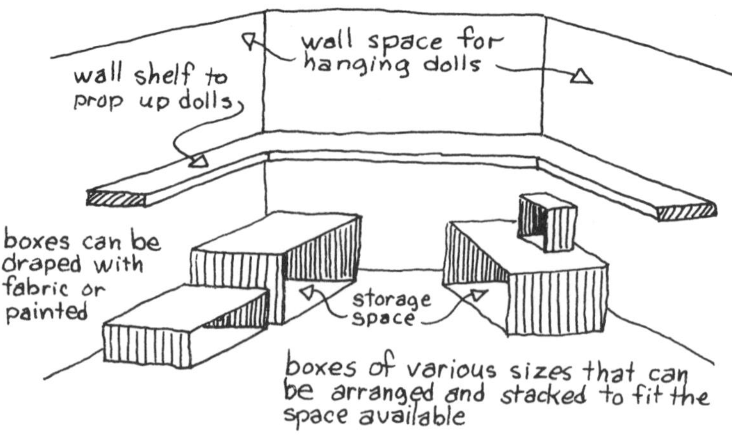

Pricing

I sold my first batch of dolls between $8 and $12. Everyone at the sale gasped, telling me that they were way underpriced. Rather than raising the prices on these dolls, I created new types of dolls and raised the prices on these, from $12 to $18. People still gasped and I realized the dolls were still underpriced. You can sell a well-crafted doll anywhere between $20 and $50 without feeling guilty or greedy. Don't be hesitant. You have used your talent to create these dolls.

I sometimes get attached to one doll. In such instances, I charge what I think the doll is worth to me. The price in no way reflects materials and time, just a large sum of money which will make the loss of the doll easier to take.

Mass Production

You will need dependable workers to cut, stuff and seam the dolls. You should be sure the quality of work won't go down when you have others do the work for you. Hire good people and check occasionally to see that their work is good.

You should estimate the number of dolls you can put out in a week, taking into account the number of workers you can get and the size of your working space. Don't overestimate your capacities.

Finally, for the sake of sanity, you will need a prototype of a doll which won't drive you crazy when you produce it again and again. You should also tell your retail outlets you may substitute one type of doll for another, if the spontaneity goes out of your dollmaking.

At present, I mass produce dolls for a shop called Mobilia in Boston and another called Pleasure Island in Poughkeepsie. I do a certain number of pieces each month for these two shops. The relationship is enjoyable because both places understand that I may substitute new dolls if I become dry in certain styles. I really can't stand seeing a doll that looks as though it had been made a thousand times already.

When you mass produce dolls, you have to calculate your charges differently. You should decide costs of materials plus time for making and selling dolls, cost of gas, shipping, and all other expenses. And you must charge of course for your own talent.

On the other hand, you should remember that the retail store is taking over the hassle of selling your dolls for you. And you will be saving on the costs of raw materials, since you will be buying in bulk. You will also have a resale number (obtainable from the Sales Tax Bureau of your state) so that you will not have to pay taxes on the stuff you buy. Generally a fair price to the stores is 50% of the usual retail costs.

This is not a firm rule. When you are selling on this level, you will have to figure out the terms of the deals yourself. Each relationship, each store, is different.

One final piece of advice: if you have only a few dolls to sell and if the store owner has to be persuaded to take your work, consignment is okay. However, if you have a large number of dolls to sell and the store owner already has proof that your dolls will sell in the store, you should be paid either immediately or at the end of thirty days.

12

Supplies and Sources

TRACING PAPER to trace drawings. A pad, 8 1/2" x 11", may be purchased at an artists' supply store.

CARBON PAPER to transfer patterns from tracing paper to heavy paper.

HEAVY PAPER for patterns. Recycle heavy, brown or white supermarket bags. Simply cut them open and iron flat.

GRAPH PAPER to enlarge or reduce patterns. Artists' supply stores carry graph paper with ¼" and ½" squares. Some fabric stores carry paper with 1" square grids.

SCISSORS, two pairs, one for paper, the other for cloth. Cutting paper will make scissors too dull to cut cloth efficiently. You might tie red cloth to the fabric scissors and tape a bit of brown masking tape to the paper scissors for quick identification.

POLYESTER FIBERFILL for stuffing dolls. It has resiliency and bounce. Small quantities can be purchased at Woolworth's. Large quantities, 100 lb. or more, from Fairfield Processing Corp. 88 Rose Hill Ave., Danbury, Conn. 06810. Ask for their brand name, Poly-Fil. You can also order from Craft Product Division, Buffalo Batt & Felt Corp., 3307 Walden Ave., Depew, N.Y. 14043.

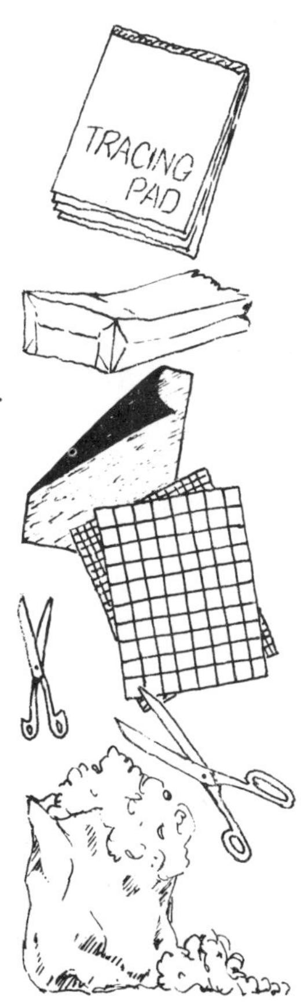

POLYESTER BATTING to quilt hands or other parts of the doll's body. Batting can be bought in small quantities at Woolworth's or in large quantities from the two companies listed under "Polyester Fiberfill."

NEEDLES & THREAD for sewing dolls and embroidering. Get a wide assortment and keep them organized. Don't forget to buy neutral colored thread to match unbleached muslin.

PINS, straight pins.

FABRIC & TRIMS for dressing dolls. Use cloth from items found at rummage sales, Goodwill shops, Salvation Army shops, and so on. Keep a large selection on hand. You will also need several yards of closely woven, unbleached muslin. For trims, look carefully at underwear and dresses in used clothing shops. You may find some interesting things.

DRAWING PEN for faces and other details. I use a Staedler fountain pen, no. 700 with a .30/00 point, bought at an artists' supply store. To prevent the point from clogging, use Mars ink. (Use ink specifically made for technical pens only.)

BRUSHES, an assortment of small brushes from Woolworth's or an artists' supply store.

YARNS & FLEECE for doll's hair. I generally use unspun wool (fleece) or handspun wool which has an interesting texture ranging from tight to loose. Commercially spun wool is very regular in texture. By the way, if you get interested in spinning your own wool, the least expensive way to begin is to buy a drop spindle for about $5, not a spinning wheel. You can buy a variety of yarns, including fleece, mail order, at The Sheepish Grin, 35 Rockleigh Terrace, Trenton, New Jersey. A friend of mine, Laurel Scheeler, runs it--she can help you a lot. You can also use recycled materials such as human hair, furs, or fake furs for dolls' hair.

Another source for wool fiber and yarns is Meg Swansen. She and her mother, Elizabeth Zimmermann, have a mail order business selling some of the most beautiful wools with wonderful textures and rich colors I've ever seen. If you prefer yarn for hair, it is worth sending 50¢ for their sample card. Meg Swansen, Pittsville, Wisconsin, 54466.

OTHER RECYCLED MATERIALS to use on dolls. You can really get inspiration from old costume jewelry, feathers, ribbons and laces, buttons, kids' shoes, hats, flowers, bows, old glasses, Christmas decorations, hankerchiefs--the list is endless. You can buy whole boxes of underwear from the Salvation Army and rummage through it when you need lace to trim a doll. Please remember that if the doll is to be for a child, detachable items (buttons, beads, etc.) should not be used.

DYES for coloring fleece for dolls' hair. RIT, found at any store.

TEXTILE PAINTS for dolls' clothing and faces. Use Versitex or Decca Paints. Buy Versitex from an artists' supply store or mail order from Dharma Trading, PO Box 1288, Berkeley, Calif. 94710. Decca from Decca Paints, 470 Maylin St., Pasadena, Calif. Dharma Trading carries a wide variety of crafts supplies.

SURGICAL GLOVES to protect your hands when dying fleece. Buy from Dharma Trading, address above.

GLAUBER SALTS used as a fixative in rainbow dying. You can buy this at a photographic supplies store. It is also sold by The Sheepish Grin. (See Yarns & Fleece section on page 92.)

About
the Author

Born in Manhattan, Loretta Pompilio attended the School of Visual Arts there. In 1974, she moved to Trumansburg, New York, and shortly thereafter began making dolls which she sells under the trade name of *Lovely Ladies and Friends*. Her larger dolls and wall pieces have been exhibited in art galleries in various cities on the East Coast and at the Hinkley Museum in Ithaca, New York. She lives with her husband, Raymond, a professional photographer, and her two sons, Julian and Jesse.